WEDNESDAY

IS

SPAGHETTI

and Macaroni and Fettuccine and Pasta Salads and More

• • •

TIME
LIFE
CUSTOM
PUBLISHING

TIME-LIFE BOOKS, ALEXANDRIA, VIRGINIA

TIME-LIFE BOOKS IS A DIVISION OF TIME LIFE INC.

PRESIDENT and CEO, Time Life Inc.   John M. Fahey Jr.
PRESIDENT, Time-Life Books   John D. Hall

TIME-LIFE CUSTOM PUBLISHING
VICE PRESIDENT and PUBLISHER   Terry Newell
Director of Sales   Neil Levin
Director of New Product Development   Regina Hall
Managing Editor   Donia Ann Steele
Editorial Director   Jennifer Pearce
Senior Art Director   Christopher M. Register
Sales Manager   Liz Ziehl
Retail Promotions Manager   Gary Stoiber
Associate Marketing Manager   Dana A. Coleman
Retail Operations Manager   Valerie Lewis
Director of Financial Operations   J. Brian Birky
Financial Analyst   Trish Palini
Production Manager   Carolyn Bounds
Quality Assurance Manager   James D. King
Executive Assistant   Tammy York

Illustrations: William Neeper

Produced by Rebus, Inc.
New York, New York

Library of Congress Cataloging-in-Publication Data
Wednesday is spaghetti and macaroni and fettucine and pasta salads and more.
p. cm. -- (The everyday cookbooks)
Includes index.
ISBN 0-8094-9188-5
1. Cookery (Pasta) 2. Quick and easy cookery. I. Time-Life Books.
II. Series.
TX809.M17W43   1995
641.8'22--dc20
95-10416
CIP

Introduction

Remember when you could tell what day of the week it was by what Mom was making for dinner? It was predictable, and comforting, and—as far as Mom was concerned—efficient. But every now and then, didn't you wish she would give her usual spaghetti recipe a rest and try something new? Now here's a cookbook that not only helps you plan meals like Mom used to make but gives you a wonderful variety of recipes, too. With *Wednesday Is Spaghetti,* you can offer your family a delightfully different pasta meal every week.

To make life even easier, this cookbook includes the following features:

- There are no difficult techniques or exotic ingredients. All of the recipes can be made with supermarket-available foods and a great many of them can be made entirely with ingredients already in the pantry.

- Each recipe is designed with everyone's busy schedule in mind, with most taking under 30 minutes to prepare. These recipes are labeled "Extra-Quick" and are marked with this symbol: ◆ (A full listing of the extra-quick recipes is included in the index under the heading Extra-Quick.)

- Many of the recipes include lower-fat alternatives, such as reduced-fat sour cream and low-fat milk. In addition, we have created a number of recipes that get fewer than 30 percent of their calories from fat. These recipes are labeled "Low-Fat" and are marked with this symbol: ◇ (A full listing of the low-fat recipes is included in the index under the heading Low-Fat.)

- As a further help to the cook, there are notes throughout the book that provide simple variations on recipes, cooking shortcuts or tips on how to lower fat, suggestions for simple desserts that can be made for weekday meals, and substitutions, in case you can't find (or don't like) certain ingredients.

- In a special section called "Family Favorites," we include recipes that even the pickiest eaters will like, such as Macaroni and Cheddar Bake and Shrimp Scampi over Linguine.

But best of all, in *Wednesday Is Spaghetti* there are enough delicious pasta recipes for more than two years' worth of Wednesdays!

Contents

PASTA WITH MEAT

PASTA SALADS

FAMILY FAVORITES

INDEX

SPAGHETTI WITH NO-COOK HERB TOMATO SAUCE

SERVES 4

◆ EXTRA-QUICK ◇ LOW-FAT

½ CUP (PACKED) FRESH BASIL LEAVES

ONE 14½-OUNCE CAN NO-SALT-ADDED
WHOLE TOMATOES, DRAINED

6 MEDIUM PLUM TOMATOES,
QUARTERED

¼ CUP PITTED BLACK OLIVES
(OPTIONAL)

2 TABLESPOONS OLIVE OIL

1 TABLESPOON FRESH LEMON JUICE

2 TEASPOONS GRATED LEMON ZEST

½ TEASPOON SALT

¼ TEASPOON BLACK PEPPER

¾ POUND SPAGHETTI OR LINGUINE

3 GARLIC CLOVES, PEELED

½ POUND SMOKED TURKEY, CUT INTO
SMALL CUBES

1. In a food processor, process the basil until coarsely chopped. Add the canned tomatoes and pulse until coarsely chopped. Add the plum tomatoes and olives (if using), and pulse until finely chopped.

2. Transfer the tomato mixture to a large serving bowl. Add the oil, lemon juice, lemon zest, salt, and pepper. Let the tomato sauce stand while you cook the pasta.

3. In a large pot of boiling water, cook the pasta with the garlic until the pasta is al dente according to package directions.

4. Drain the pasta and garlic. Press the cooked garlic through a garlic press (or mash it with a fork), add it to the tomato sauce, and stir to blend. Add the pasta and turkey, and toss to combine.

Substitution: *This fresh-tasting no-cook tomato sauce is best made in the summer, at the height of tomato and basil season. However, when fresh tomatoes and basil are unavailable, you can substitute 9 drained whole tomatoes in place of the fresh, and 1 tablespoon dried basil in place of the fresh. Add the dried basil along with the olive oil and lemon juice in Step 2.*

Spinach Gnocchi with Marinara Sauce

SERVES 4

1 TABLESPOON OLIVE OIL

1 SMALL ONION, COARSELY CHOPPED

4 GARLIC CLOVES, MINCED

ONE 14½-OUNCE CAN NO-SALT-ADDED
WHOLE TOMATOES

1 TEASPOON OREGANO

1 TABLESPOON UNSALTED BUTTER

ONE 10-OUNCE PACKAGE FROZEN
CHOPPED SPINACH, THAWED AND
SQUEEZED DRY

4 SCALLIONS, COARSELY CHOPPED

½ CUP PART-SKIM RICOTTA CHEESE

1 EGG

½ CUP FLOUR

½ CUP GRATED PARMESAN CHEESE

¼ TEASPOON SALT

¼ TEASPOON BLACK PEPPER

1. In a medium saucepan, warm the oil over medium-high heat. Add the onion and half of the garlic, and cook, stirring frequently, until the onion begins to brown, about 5 minutes. Add the tomatoes and oregano and break up the tomatoes with the back of a spoon. Bring to a boil, reduce the heat to low, cover, and simmer the marinara sauce while you prepare the gnocchi.

2. In another medium saucepan, melt the butter over medium-high heat. Add the spinach, scallions, and remaining garlic. Cook, stirring constantly, until the scallions begin to soften, about 2 minutes.

3. Add the ricotta and cook until the mixture loses some of its moisture and begins to bind together, about 3 minutes. Remove from the heat and beat in the egg. Mix in the flour, Parmesan, salt, and pepper.

4. With floured hands, using a scant 1 tablespoon for each, form the ricotta mixture into balls. Place the gnocchi in a single layer on a plate, cover loosely with plastic wrap, and freeze until slightly firm, about 15 minutes. Meanwhile, bring a large pot of water to a boil.

5. Add the gnocchi to the boiling water and cook until they float to the top, 5 to 8 minutes. With a slotted spoon, transfer the gnocchi to a colander to drain. Spoon the sauce into 4 shallow bowls, place several gnocchi on top, and serve hot.

Vermicelli with Smoky Tomato Sauce

SERVES 4

4 SLICES BACON

2 TABLESPOONS OLIVE OIL

1 MEDIUM ONION, COARSELY CHOPPED

3 GARLIC CLOVES, MINCED

¾ POUND VERMICELLI OR SPAGHETTINI

¼ CUP DRY RED WINE OR BEEF BROTH

ONE 14½-OUNCE CAN NO-SALT-ADDED
   WHOLE TOMATOES

ONE 8-OUNCE CAN TOMATO SAUCE

1 BAY LEAF

2 TABLESPOONS MINCED FRESH BASIL,
   OR 1 TEASPOON DRIED

¼ TEASPOON BLACK PEPPER

¼ CUP CHOPPED CILANTRO OR PARSLEY

1. In a large skillet, cook the bacon over medium heat until crisp, about 10 minutes. Drain the bacon on paper towels, crumble, and set aside.

2. Drain off the bacon fat and wipe out the skillet with paper towels. Add the oil to the skillet and warm over medium heat. Add the onion and garlic, and cook, stirring frequently, until the onion is softened, about 5 minutes.

3. In a large pot of boiling water, cook the pasta until al dente according to package directions.

4. Meanwhile, add the wine to the skillet and cook for 1 minute. Add the tomatoes, breaking them up with the back of a spoon. Stir in the tomato sauce, bay leaf, basil, and pepper. Bring to a boil, reduce the heat to medium-low, cover, and simmer until the sauce is slightly thickened, 10 to 12 minutes.

5. Drain the pasta and transfer it to a large bowl. Remove and discard the bay leaf from the sauce, pour the sauce on top of the pasta, and toss to combine. Divide the mixture among 4 shallow bowls, sprinkle with the crumbled bacon and cilantro, and serve at once.

Linguine with Mediterranean Pasta Sauce

SERVES 4

◇ LOW-FAT

1 TABLESPOON OLIVE OIL

1 GARLIC CLOVE, MINCED

ONE 28-OUNCE CAN NO-SALT-ADDED
WHOLE TOMATOES, DRAINED

6 BLACK OLIVES, PREFERABLY OIL-
CURED, PITTED AND CUT INTO
STRIPS

2 TEASPOONS CAPERS (OPTIONAL),
RINSED AND CHOPPED

¼ TEASPOON SALT

⅛ TEASPOON RED PEPPER FLAKES

1 TEASPOON CHOPPED FRESH
OREGANO, OR ½ TEASPOON DRIED

½ POUND LINGUINE

2 TABLESPOONS GRATED ROMANO
CHEESE

1. In a large nonstick skillet, warm the oil over medium heat. Add the garlic and cook, stirring frequently, until fragrant, about 30 seconds.

2. Add the tomatoes and break them up with a spoon. Stir in the olives, capers (if using), salt, and red pepper flakes. Reduce the heat to low, partially cover, and simmer until the mixture is slightly thickened, about 20 minutes. Stir in the oregano, partially cover, and cook for 10 minutes.

3. Meanwhile, in a large pot of boiling water, cook the pasta until al dente according to package directions.

4. Drain the pasta, add it to the tomato-olive sauce, and toss well to coat. Divide the pasta mixture among 4 shallow bowls and sprinkle with the Romano.

Variation: *To give this the distinct and aromatic flavors of southern France, substitute 1 teaspoon of fennel seeds for the oregano and add 2 teaspoons of grated orange zest in Step 2.*

FETTUCCINE WITH PECAN ALFREDO SAUCE

SERVES 4

♦ EXTRA-QUICK

½ POUND FETTUCCINE

1 GARLIC CLOVE, PEELED

¼ CUP (PACKED) FRESH BASIL LEAVES

½ CUP PECAN HALVES OR PIECES,
TOASTED

¼ CUP GRATED PARMESAN CHEESE

¼ TEASPOON SALT

⅛ TEASPOON BLACK PEPPER

2 TABLESPOONS OLIVE OIL

¼ CUP HALF-AND-HALF

¼ CUP PLAIN LOW-FAT YOGURT

1. In a large pot of boiling water, cook the pasta until al dente according to package directions.

2. Meanwhile, in a food processor or blender, process the garlic until minced. Add the basil and process until finely chopped. Add the pecans, Parmesan, salt, and pepper, and process just until the pecans are evenly chopped.

3. With the machine running, gradually add the oil until combined. Add the half-and-half and yogurt, and process to blend.

4. Drain the pasta and transfer it to a large serving bowl. Add the pecan alfredo sauce and toss until thoroughly coated.

KITCHEN NOTE: *When creamy alfredo sauce meets Genovese pesto, the result is an extraordinary topping for pasta. This streamlined version of an alfredo sauce—made with yogurt and half-and-half in place of the traditional heavy cream—is enriched with toasted pecans, basil, garlic, and grated Parmesan for an irresistible flavor and a luxurious texture.*

Penne with Creamy Ricotta Sauce

SERVES 4

◆ EXTRA-QUICK ◇ LOW-FAT

1 POUND PENNE OR OTHER SHORT
   TUBULAR PASTA
3 LARGE CELERY RIBS, COARSELY
   CHOPPED
¾ CUP REDUCED-FAT SOUR CREAM
¾ CUP PLAIN LOW-FAT YOGURT
½ CUP PART-SKIM RICOTTA CHEESE
½ TEASPOON NUTMEG

½ TEASPOON SALT
¼ TEASPOON BLACK PEPPER
1 TABLESPOON OLIVE OIL
½ CUP FINELY CHOPPED SHALLOTS
   OR SCALLION WHITES
¼ CUP FINELY CHOPPED PARSLEY
3 TABLESPOONS FRESH LIME JUICE

1. In a large pot of boiling water, cook the pasta until al dente according to package directions.

2. Meanwhile, steam the celery until tender but still firm, 3 to 4 minutes.

3. In a small bowl, combine the sour cream, yogurt, and ricotta. Stir in the nutmeg, salt, and pepper. Set aside.

4. In a large nonstick skillet, warm the oil over medium heat. Add the celery, shallots, and parsley, and cook, stirring frequently, until the shallots are tender, about 5 minutes.

5. Drain the pasta well and stir it into the celery mixture. Remove the pan from the heat and gently stir in the sour cream mixture.

6. Return the pan to low heat, cover, and warm the pasta mixture, stirring occasionally, until thoroughly heated, about 3 minutes. Stir in the lime juice and serve at once.

Spaghetti with Fresh Basil, Pine Nuts, and Cheese

SERVES 4

◆ EXTRA-QUICK

¾ POUND SPAGHETTI

1 TABLESPOON OLIVE OIL

1 GARLIC CLOVE, MINCED

1 CUP SHREDDED FRESH BASIL LEAVES

½ CUP CHICKEN BROTH

½ CUP GRATED ROMANO CHEESE

¼ CUP PINE NUTS, TOASTED

¼ TEASPOON SALT

¼ TEASPOON BLACK PEPPER

1. In a large pot of boiling water, cook the pasta until al dente according to package directions.

2. Meanwhile, in a medium nonstick skillet, warm the oil over medium heat. Add the garlic and cook, stirring constantly, until fragrant, about 30 seconds.

3. Reduce the heat to low, stir in the basil, and cook until wilted, about 30 seconds. Add the broth and simmer, stirring occasionally, until the flavors are blended, about 10 minutes.

4. Drain the pasta, add it to the skillet, and toss well to coat. Add the Romano, pine nuts, salt, and pepper, and toss again. Serve hot.

SWEET AFTERTHOUGHT: *For a simple dessert, serve homemade rum raisin ice cream. Just stir ⅔ cup chopped golden raisins, ¼ cup chopped walnuts (or pine nuts if you have any left over), 3 tablespoons of rum, and 2 tablespoons of honey into 1 quart of softened store-bought vanilla or chocolate ice cream. Refreeze the ice cream until ready to serve, then let soften slightly before serving.*

Pasta with Three Cheeses

SERVES 4

◆ EXTRA-QUICK

1 POUND ELBOW MACARONI OR SMALL
   PASTA SHELLS

1 CUP BROCCOLI FLORETS

12 CHERRY TOMATOES, HALVED

1 CUP PITTED OIL-CURED BLACK
   OLIVES (OPTIONAL)

3 TABLESPOONS UNSALTED BUTTER

5 LARGE MUSHROOMS, THINLY SLICED

¼ TEASPOON BLACK PEPPER

¼ CUP OLIVE OIL

3 TABLESPOONS CHOPPED FRESH BASIL,
   OR 2 TEASPOONS DRIED

1½ TABLESPOONS FRESH LEMON JUICE

1 TABLESPOON CHOPPED PARSLEY

1 TEASPOON RED WINE VINEGAR

½ TEASPOON MINCED GARLIC

¼ POUND BLUE CHEESE OR SOFT GOAT
   CHEESE, CRUMBLED

¼ CUP GRATED PARMESAN CHEESE

¼ CUP GRATED ROMANO CHEESE

1. In a large pot of boiling water, cook the pasta until al dente according to package directions. Drain and rinse under cold running water.

2. Meanwhile, in a medium saucepan of boiling water, blanch the broccoli for 1 minute. Drain and rinse under cold running water. In a large serving bowl, combine the broccoli, tomatoes, and olives (if using).

3. In a medium skillet, melt the butter over medium heat. Add the mushrooms and pepper, and cook, stirring frequently, until the mushrooms start to give up their liquid, 3 to 4 minutes. Add the mushrooms to the broccoli mixture.

4. In a food processor or blender, combine the oil, basil, lemon juice, parsley, vinegar, and garlic, and process until smooth.

5. Add the pasta to the broccoli-mushroom mixture. Add the blue cheese, Parmesan, and Romano, and toss to combine. Add the basil-lemon sauce and toss gently until evenly coated. Serve at room temperature.

Savory Pasta-Cheese Casserole with Sweet Peppers

SERVES 4

¾ POUND MEDIUM PASTA SHELLS
1 MEDIUM RED BELL PEPPER, CUT
   INTO THIN STRIPS
1 MEDIUM GREEN BELL PEPPER, CUT
   INTO THIN STRIPS
1 GARLIC CLOVE, PEELED
2 CUPS LOW-FAT COTTAGE CHEESE

3 OUNCES NEUFCHÂTEL CREAM CHEESE
½ CUP LOW-FAT MILK
¼ TEASPOON NUTMEG
¼ TEASPOON SALT
¼ TEASPOON BLACK PEPPER
½ CUP GRATED PARMESAN CHEESE
½ CUP GRATED ROMANO CHEESE

1. Preheat the oven to 375°. Butter a 2-quart baking dish.

2. In a large pot of boiling water, cook the pasta until al dente according to package directions. About 3 minutes before the pasta is done, add the bell peppers to the boiling water and cook until they begin to soften.

3. Meanwhile, in a food processor or blender, process the garlic until minced. Add the cottage cheese and cream cheese, and blend until the mixture is smooth. Blend in the milk, nutmeg, salt, and black pepper.

4. In a small bowl, blend the Parmesan and Romano cheeses.

5. Drain the pasta and bell peppers well and transfer them to a large bowl. Add the cottage cheese mixture and ¾ cup of the Parmesan-Romano mixture, and toss gently to combine.

6. Spoon the mixture into the prepared baking dish. Sprinkle the casserole with the remaining ¼ cup Parmesan-Romano mixture and bake for 25 to 30 minutes, or until golden on top.

Red, Gold, and Green Skillet "Casserole"

SERVES 4 TO 6

◆ EXTRA-QUICK

1 TABLESPOON OLIVE OIL

1 TABLESPOON UNSALTED BUTTER

1 MEDIUM ONION, COARSELY CHOPPED

2 GARLIC CLOVES, MINCED

4 MEDIUM PLUM TOMATOES, COARSELY CHOPPED

1 MEDIUM GREEN BELL PEPPER, COARSELY CHOPPED

2 CUPS CHICKEN BROTH, PREFERABLY REDUCED-SODIUM

ONE 4-OUNCE CAN CHOPPED MILD GREEN CHILIES, DRAINED

½ TEASPOON OREGANO

¼ TEASPOON BLACK PEPPER

½ POUND DITALINI PASTA OR OTHER SMALL, TUBULAR PASTA

1½ CUPS SHREDDED MONTEREY JACK CHEESE

1. In a large ovenproof skillet, warm the oil with the butter over medium-high heat until the butter is melted. Add the onion and garlic, and cook, stirring frequently, until the onion begins to brown, about 5 minutes.

2. Preheat the broiler.

3. Stir the tomatoes, bell pepper, broth, green chilies, oregano, and black pepper into the skillet. Bring to a boil over high heat and add the pasta. Reduce the heat to low, cover, and simmer, stirring frequently, until the pasta is al dente, about 9 minutes. Remove from the heat.

4. Stir in 1 cup of the cheese. Sprinkle the remaining ½ cup cheese evenly over the top. Place the skillet under the broiler and broil 4 inches from the heat for 3 to 5 minutes, or until golden brown on top.

SUBSTITUTIONS: *For a milder dish, substitute a second bell pepper for the canned green chilies. Or, for added "heat," use pepper jack cheese for the regular Monterey jack—or simply add a minced fresh or pickled jalapeño pepper.*

PASTA WHEELS WiTH MiXED VEGETABLES AnD PARmESAn

SERVES 4

◆ EXTRA - QUiCK

4 TABLESPOONS UNSALTED BUTTER

2 MEDIUM LEEKS, TRIMMED, WELL CLEANED, AND FINELY CHOPPED

1 POUND WAGON WHEEL PASTA OR MEDIUM PASTA SHELLS

1 MEDIUM ZUCCHINI, THINLY SLICED

¼ POUND MUSHROOMS, THINLY SLICED

1 LARGE TOMATO, CHOPPED

1 CUP HALF-AND-HALF

1 CUP GRATED PARMESAN CHEESE

¼ TEASPOON SALT

¼ TEASPOON BLACK PEPPER

1. In a medium skillet, melt the butter over medium heat. Add the leeks and cook, stirring occasionally, until they are softened, about 10 minutes.

2. Meanwhile, in a large pot of boiling water, cook the pasta until al dente according to package directions.

3. Increase the heat under the skillet to medium-high. Add the zucchini, mushrooms, and tomato, and stir-fry until the zucchini is barely tender, about 2 minutes.

4. Stir in the half-and-half, ½ cup of the Parmesan, the salt, and pepper. Just before the mixture comes to a boil, remove the pan from the heat.

5. Drain the pasta and transfer it to a large serving bowl. Spoon the vegetable sauce on top and toss well to combine. Pass the remaining Parmesan at the table.

SUBSTITUTION: *Although leeks add a wonderfully mild onion flavor, this dish can be made with onions instead. Use 1 large onion, preferably a sweet variety such as Vidalia, Maui, or Walla Walla.*

Noodles with Creamy Poppy Seed Sauce

SERVES 4

◆ EXTRA-QUICK

2 TABLESPOONS VEGETABLE OIL

2 MEDIUM ONIONS, THINLY SLICED

2 GARLIC CLOVES, MINCED

2 TABLESPOONS UNSALTED BUTTER

½ POUND MUSHROOMS, THINLY SLICED

⅓ CUP FRESH LEMON JUICE

¾ TEASPOON SALT

½ TEASPOON BLACK PEPPER

PINCH OF CAYENNE PEPPER

¾ POUND WIDE EGG NOODLES

⅓ CUP REDUCED-FAT SOUR CREAM

⅓ CUP PLAIN LOW-FAT YOGURT

2 TABLESPOONS POPPY SEEDS

1 TABLESPOON GRATED LEMON ZEST

1. In a medium skillet, warm the oil over medium-high heat. Add the onions and garlic, and cook, stirring frequently, until the onions begin to brown, about 5 minutes.

2. Add the butter and warm until melted. Add the mushrooms and cook, stirring frequently, until they begin to soften, about 5 minutes.

3. Add the lemon juice, salt, and black and cayenne peppers, and bring the mixture to a boil. Reduce the heat to very low, cover, and keep warm while you cook the noodles.

4. In a large pot of boiling water, cook the noodles until al dente according to package directions.

5. Meanwhile, in a small bowl, combine the sour cream, yogurt, poppy seeds, and lemon zest.

6. Drain the noodles and transfer them to a large serving bowl. Add the mushroom mixture and the sour cream mixture and toss well to combine.

FETTUCCINE WITH SPINACH-PARMESAN SAUCE

SERVES 4

♦ EXTRA-QUICK

3 GARLIC CLOVES, PEELED

¼ CUP (PACKED) PARSLEY SPRIGS

½ CUP GRATED PARMESAN CHEESE

¼ CUP WALNUT PIECES

1 TEASPOON SALT

¼ TEASPOON BLACK PEPPER

½ CUP OLIVE OIL

¼ CUP CHICKEN BROTH

ONE 10-OUNCE PACKAGE FROZEN SPINACH, THAWED AND SQUEEZED DRY

¾ POUND FETTUCCINE OR OTHER BROAD NOODLES

1. In a food processor or blender, process the garlic and parsley until minced. Add the Parmesan, walnuts, salt, and pepper, and pulse to blend.

2. Add the oil and broth and then the spinach, and pulse until a smooth purée forms.

3. In a large pot of boiling water, cook the pasta until al dente according to package directions.

4. Drain the pasta well and transfer it to a large serving bowl. Add the spinach-Parmesan sauce, toss to coat, and serve.

SWEET AFTERTHOUGHT: *Cut 4 nectarines in half and remove the pits. Place the nectarine halves in a broilerproof dish and fill the nectarine cavities with a small nugget of butter, some brown sugar, and (if desired) a splash of amaretto liqueur. Broil until the sugar-butter mixture is melted and bubbling. For a real treat, serve the broiled fruit with a scoop of vanilla ice cream.*

Fettuccine with Mushroom-Pesto Cream

SERVES 4

♦ EXTRA-QUICK

1 TABLESPOON VEGETABLE OIL

1 MEDIUM ONION, COARSELY CHOPPED

3 GARLIC CLOVES, MINCED

¾ POUND FETTUCCINE

2 TABLESPOONS UNSALTED BUTTER

½ POUND MUSHROOMS, THINLY SLICED

1 TABLESPOON BASIL

ONE 10-OUNCE PACKAGE FROZEN
CHOPPED SPINACH, THAWED AND
SQUEEZED DRY

1½ CUPS REDUCED-FAT SOUR CREAM

½ CUP GRATED PARMESAN CHEESE

½ TEASPOON SALT

¼ TEASPOON BLACK PEPPER

1. In a large skillet, warm the oil over medium-high heat. Add the onion and garlic, and cook, stirring frequently, until the mixture is golden, about 5 minutes.

2. In a large pot of boiling water, cook the pasta until al dente according to package directions.

3. Meanwhile, add the butter to the skillet and heat until melted. Reduce the heat to medium, add the mushrooms, and cook until the mushrooms are wilted, about 5 minutes.

4. Stir in the basil and spinach, and cook, stirring frequently, until heated through, about 1 minute. Reduce the heat to low and stir in the sour cream, Parmesan, salt, and pepper. Cook, stirring constantly, just until the mixture is heated through, about 1 minute. Remove the skillet from the heat.

5. Drain the pasta and transfer it to a large serving bowl. Add the mushroom-pesto cream, toss to coat, and serve.

Linguine with Savory Mushroom-Wine Sauce

SERVES 4

♦ EXTRA-QUICK

¼ CUP OLIVE OIL

2½ TEASPOONS MINCED GARLIC

1½ POUNDS MUSHROOMS, THINLY
 SLICED

½ CUP DRY WHITE WINE OR REDUCED-
 SODIUM CHICKEN BROTH

2 TEASPOONS FRESH LEMON JUICE

½ TEASPOON SALT

1 POUND LINGUINE OR FETTUCCINE

2 TEASPOONS MINCED PARSLEY

¼ TEASPOON BLACK PEPPER

1. In a large nonstick skillet, warm 2 tablespoons of the oil over medium heat. Stir in the garlic and cook, stirring frequently, until fragrant, about 2 minutes. Add the mushrooms and cook, stirring, until they exude their liquid, about 5 minutes.

2. Add the wine, lemon juice, and salt. Bring to a simmer and cook, stirring frequently, until the liquid evaporates, about 15 minutes.

3. Meanwhile, in a large pot of boiling water, cook the pasta until al dente according to package directions.

4. Drain the pasta in a colander. Add the remaining 2 tablespoons oil to the pasta cooking pot and warm over low heat. Return the pasta to the pot and toss gently to coat. Continue tossing until any excess liquid evaporates and the pasta begins to separate, 1 to 1½ minutes.

5. Stir the parsley and pepper into the mushroom sauce.

6. Divide the pasta among 4 plates, spoon the mushroom sauce on top, and serve.

Penne with Tomatoes, Mushrooms, and Tarragon

SERVES 4

◇ LOW-FAT

½ OUNCE DRIED MUSHROOMS

1 CUP BOILING WATER

2 TABLESPOONS OLIVE OIL

1 SMALL ONION, FINELY CHOPPED

½ POUND FRESH BUTTON MUSHROOMS, DICED

½ TEASPOON SALT

¼ TEASPOON BLACK PEPPER

3 GARLIC CLOVES, MINCED

1 CUP DRY WHITE WINE OR REDUCED-SODIUM CHICKEN BROTH

½ POUND PENNE OR OTHER SHORT, TUBULAR PASTA

1½ POUNDS TOMATOES, CHOPPED

⅓ CUP CHOPPED PARSLEY

2 TABLESPOONS CHOPPED FRESH TARRAGON, OR 2 TEASPOONS DRIED

1. In a small bowl, combine the dried mushrooms and the boiling water and set aside to soak until softened, about 10 minutes. Reserving the soaking liquid, drain the mushrooms and cut them into small dice.

2. In a large skillet, warm the oil over medium heat. Add the onion and cook, stirring frequently, until softened, about 4 minutes. Add the dried and fresh mushrooms, salt, and pepper. Cook until the mushrooms begin to brown, about 5 minutes. Stir in the garlic and wine, and cook the mixture until the liquid is reduced to approximately 2 tablespoons, about 5 minutes.

3. Meanwhile, in a large pot of boiling water, cook the pasta until al dente according to package directions.

4. Pour the reserved mushroom soaking liquid (carefully leaving any grit behind in the bowl) into the skillet and cook until the liquid is reduced to approximately ¼ cup, about 5 minutes. Stir in the tomatoes and cook until heated through, about 3 minutes.

5. Drain the pasta and add it to the skillet along with the parsley and tarragon. Toss well to combine, and serve.

DOUBLE-MUSHROOM BOW TIES

SERVES 4

1 CUP CHICKEN BROTH, PREFERABLY
   REDUCED-SODIUM
1 OUNCE DRIED MUSHROOMS
2 TABLESPOONS OLIVE OIL
4 TABLESPOONS UNSALTED BUTTER
1 MEDIUM ONION, THINLY SLICED
3 GARLIC CLOVES, MINCED
¾ POUND FRESH BUTTON MUSHROOMS,
   THINLY SLICED

2 TEASPOONS OREGANO
PINCH OF SALT
¼ TEASPOON BLACK PEPPER
¾ POUND BOW TIE PASTA OR OTHER
   FANCY PASTA SHAPE
⅓ CUP GRATED PARMESAN CHEESE

1. In a small saucepan, bring the broth to a boil. In a large measuring cup, combine the dried mushrooms and the boiling broth. Let the mushrooms soak until softened, about 10 minutes.

2. Meanwhile, in a large skillet, warm the oil with 2 tablespoons of the butter over medium-high heat until the butter is melted. Add the onion and garlic, and cook, stirring frequently, until the onion begins to brown, about 5 minutes.

3. Add the fresh mushrooms and stir-fry until the mushrooms begin to wilt, 1 to 2 minutes.

4. Stir in the dried mushrooms and ½ cup of their soaking liquid (carefully leaving any grit behind in the measuring cup). Add the oreg-ano, salt, and pepper. Bring the mixture to a boil, reduce the heat to low, and simmer while you cook the pasta.

5. In a large pot of boiling water, cook the pasta until al dente according to package directions.

6. Drain the pasta and transfer it to a large serving bowl. Stir the remaining 2 table-spoons butter into the mushroom sauce. Spoon the mushroom sauce on top of the pasta and toss to coat. Pass the Parmesan on the side.

Couscous
with Gingered Vegetables

SERVES 4

◆ EXTRA-QUICK ◇ LOW-FAT

1 CUP QUICK-COOKING COUSCOUS

1 CUP BOILING WATER

1 TABLESPOON VEGETABLE OIL

6 SCALLIONS, WHITE PARTS FINELY
MINCED, GREEN PARTS THINLY
SLICED, PARTS KEPT SEPARATE

4 GARLIC CLOVES, MINCED

1 TABLESPOON MINCED FRESH GINGER

4 MEDIUM CARROTS, CUT INTO THIN
ROUNDS

⅛ TEASPOON RED PEPPER FLAKES

⅛ TEASPOON GROUND CORIANDER

2 CUPS CHICKEN BROTH, PREFERABLY
REDUCED-SODIUM

2 MEDIUM ZUCCHINI, CUT INTO THIN
ROUNDS

1 MEDIUM RED BELL PEPPER, CUT INTO
½-INCH SQUARES

1. In a large heatproof serving bowl, combine the couscous and the boiling water. Cover the bowl and let the couscous stand while you cook the vegetables.

2. In a large, deep skillet, warm the oil over medium-high heat. Add the scallion whites, garlic, and ginger, and cook, stirring constantly, for 1 minute.

3. Stir in the carrots, red pepper flakes, and coriander until well combined. Pour in the broth. Bring to a boil, reduce to a simmer, cover, and cook until the carrots are just tender, about 5 minutes.

4. Add the zucchini to the skillet, cover, and cook until the zucchini is barely tender, about 3 minutes. Stir in the bell pepper and scallion greens. Cook, uncovered, for 3 minutes.

5. With a fork, fluff the couscous. Spoon the vegetable mixture over the couscous, mix well, and serve.

Lemon Fettuccine with Artichokes

SERVES 4

◆ EXTRA-QUICK

2 LEMONS

½ POUND FETTUCCINE OR OTHER
BROAD NOODLES

1 TABLESPOON OLIVE OIL

1 MEDIUM ONION, COARSELY CHOPPED

2 GARLIC CLOVES, MINCED

TWO 6-OUNCE JARS MARINATED
ARTICHOKE HEARTS

1 CUP REDUCED-FAT SOUR CREAM

1 POUND PART-SKIM MOZZARELLA
CHEESE, CUT INTO ½-INCH CUBES

¼ CUP CHOPPED PARSLEY

1. Finely grate the zest of 1 of the lemons and then juice the lemon. Set the lemon zest and juice aside. Quarter the remaining lemon.

2. In a large pot of boiling water, cook the pasta with the lemon quarters until the pasta is al dente according to package directions.

3. Meanwhile, in a medium skillet, warm the oil over medium-high heat. Add the onion and garlic, and cook, stirring frequently, until the onion begins to brown, about 5 minutes.

4. Drain 1 jar of artichokes, discarding the liquid. Add the drained artichokes and the remaining jar of artichokes with their liquid

to the skillet. Cook, stirring frequently, until the artichokes are heated through, about 3 minutes.

5. Remove the skillet from the heat and stir in the sour cream and mozzarella.

6. Drain the pasta and transfer it to a large serving bowl. Remove and discard the lemon quarters. Add the artichoke sauce, the reserved lemon zest and juice, and the parsley to the pasta and toss to coat.

Angel Hair Pasta with Green Beans and Almonds

SERVES 4

2 TABLESPOONS OLIVE OIL

2 MEDIUM ONIONS, HALVED AND
   THINLY SLICED

2 GARLIC CLOVES, MINCED

½ POUND FRESH GREEN BEANS, CUT
   INTO 2-INCH LENGTHS, OR 1½ CUPS
   FROZEN CUT GREEN BEANS, THAWED

1 CUP PITTED BLACK OLIVES, HALVED
   (OPTIONAL)

½ POUND ANGEL HAIR PASTA OR
   SPAGHETTINI

ONE 14½-OUNCE CAN NO-SALT-ADDED
   WHOLE TOMATOES, DRAINED

3 TABLESPOONS CHOPPED PARSLEY

⅓ CUP SLICED ALMONDS, TOASTED

1. In a large skillet, warm the oil over medium-high heat. Add the onions and garlic, and cook, stirring frequently, until the onions are well browned, about 10 minutes. Add the green beans and olives, and cook, stirring frequently, for 3 minutes.

2. Meanwhile, in a large pot of boiling water, cook the pasta until al dente according to package directions.

3. Add the tomatoes to the skillet, breaking them up with a spoon, and cook the mixture for 2 minutes. Add the parsley and cook for 1 minute longer. Remove from the heat.

4. Drain the pasta and transfer it to a large serving bowl. Add the green bean mixture and toss well to combine. Divide the pasta among 4 plates and sprinkle with the almonds.

Variation: *To give this pasta dish a Spanish flavor, substitute pitted (or pimiento-stuffed) green olives for the black olives, but sliver them and use only ½ cup. Also use the fruitiest, most strongly flavored olive oil you have. If you like the taste of saffron, you might add a small pinch to the pasta cooking water.*

FETTUCCINE WITH VEGETABLE RIBBONS

SERVES 4

◆ EXTRA-QUICK   ◇ LOW-FAT

2 MEDIUM CARROTS

2 MEDIUM ZUCCHINI, UNPEELED

½ POUND REGULAR OR SPINACH
FETTUCCINE

1 CUP CHICKEN BROTH, PREFERABLY
REDUCED-SODIUM

2 GARLIC CLOVES, MINCED

1 TEASPOON OREGANO

¼ TEASPOON BLACK PEPPER

2 TABLESPOONS CORNSTARCH

4 SCALLIONS, COARSELY CHOPPED

¼ CUP GRATED PARMESAN CHEESE

1. Using a cheese slicer or vegetable peeler, peel the carrots and zucchini into long ribbons.

2. In a large pot of boiling water, cook the pasta until al dente according to package directions.

3. Meanwhile, in a large skillet, combine ¾ cup of the broth, the garlic, oregano, and pepper, and bring to a boil. Add the carrot and zucchini ribbons, reduce the heat to medium-low, cover, and simmer until the vegetables are tender, about 3 minutes. Remove the skillet from the heat.

4. With a slotted spoon, transfer the vegetables to a large serving bowl. Reserve the broth

mixture in the skillet. Drain the pasta and add it to the vegetable ribbons. Cover loosely with foil to keep warm.

5. In a small bowl, combine the cornstarch and the remaining ¼ cup broth, and stir to blend. Return the broth mixture in the skillet to a boil over medium-high heat, stir in the cornstarch mixture and the scallions, and cook, stirring constantly, until the sauce has thickened slightly, about 1 minute.

6. Pour the sauce over the pasta-vegetable mixture and toss to coat. Add the Parmesan, toss again, and serve at once.

ZESTY GARDEN PASTA

SERVES 4

4 TABLESPOONS UNSALTED BUTTER

3 TABLESPOONS FLOUR

1½ CUPS CHICKEN BROTH, PREFERABLY
REDUCED-SODIUM

1½ TEASPOONS OREGANO

½ TEASPOON BLACK PEPPER

PINCH OF CAYENNE PEPPER

½ POUND LINGUINE

1 TABLESPOON OLIVE OIL

1 MEDIUM ONION, THINLY SLICED

3 GARLIC CLOVES, MINCED

½ MEDIUM HEAD OF CAULIFLOWER,
CUT INTO FLORETS

2 MEDIUM STALKS BROCCOLI, CUT
INTO BITE-SIZE PIECES

ONE 10-OUNCE PACKAGE FROZEN PEAS

½ TEASPOON SALT

1 LARGE TOMATO, COARSELY CHOPPED

½ CUP SLICED PITTED BLACK OLIVES
(OPTIONAL)

½ CUP GRATED PARMESAN CHEESE

¼ CUP CHOPPED PARSLEY

1. In a small saucepan, melt 3 tablespoons of the butter over medium-high heat. Add the flour and stir until the flour is no longer visible, about 30 seconds. Stir in 1 cup of the broth, ½ teaspoon of the oregano, and the black and cayenne peppers. Bring the mixture to a boil. Reduce the heat to low, cover, and simmer, stirring occasionally, while you cook the pasta.

2. In a large pot of boiling water, cook the pasta until al dente according to package directions.

3. Meanwhile, in a large skillet, warm the oil with the remaining 1 tablespoon butter over medium-high heat until the butter is melted.

Add the onion and garlic, and cook, stirring frequently, until the mixture begins to brown, about 5 minutes.

4. Stir in the cauliflower, broccoli, peas, the remaining 1 teaspoon oregano, and the salt. Cook, stirring frequently, until the vegetables begin to soften, 3 to 5 minutes. Cover and cook until the vegetables are just crisp-tender, 1 to 2 minutes. Stir in the tomato and the remaining ½ cup broth, and stir to blend.

5. Drain the pasta and transfer it to a large serving bowl. Add the vegetable mixture, olives (if using), Parmesan, and parsley, and toss well to combine.

EGG NOODLES WITH BASIL, VEGETABLES, AND PINE NUTS

SERVES 4

◆ EXTRA - QUICK

2 TABLESPOONS OLIVE OIL

2 TABLESPOONS UNSALTED BUTTER

⅓ CUP (PACKED) FRESH BASIL LEAVES, MINCED, OR 2½ TEASPOONS DRIED BASIL

3 GARLIC CLOVES, MINCED

¾ POUND WIDE EGG NOODLES

1 TABLESPOON CHICKEN BROTH

1 TEASPOON CORNSTARCH

2 SMALL ZUCCHINI, THINLY SLICED

½ POUND MUSHROOMS, THINLY SLICED

10 CANNED NO-SALT-ADDED WHOLE TOMATOES, WELL DRAINED AND CHOPPED

½ TEASPOON SALT

¼ TEASPOON BLACK PEPPER

¼ CUP PINE NUTS, TOASTED

1. In a large skillet, warm the oil with the butter over medium-high heat until the butter is melted. Add the basil and garlic, and cook, stirring constantly, until the mixture is fragrant, about 5 minutes.

2. In a large pot of boiling water, cook the noodles until al dente according to package directions.

3. Meanwhile, in a small bowl, combine the broth and cornstarch, and stir to blend. Increase the heat under the skillet to medium-high and add the zucchini, mushrooms, and tomatoes. Stir in the cornstarch mixture and cook, stirring constantly, until the vegetables are tender and the mixture is slightly thickened, about 6 minutes. Stir in the salt and pepper, and remove from the heat.

4. Drain the noodles and transfer them to a large serving bowl. Top with the vegetable mixture and toss to combine. Sprinkle with the pine nuts and serve.

SUBSTITUTION: *You can use any type of nut—such as walnuts, almonds, or pecans—in place of the pine nuts. Just be sure to toast them (in a dry skillet or in a toaster oven) for maximum flavor. Times will vary depending on the nut, so keep an eye on them.*

Bacon, Cauliflower, and Parmesan Pasta

SERVES 4

4 SLICES BACON

2 TABLESPOONS OLIVE OIL

8 SCALLIONS, COARSELY CHOPPED

3 GARLIC CLOVES, MINCED

½ POUND RIGATONI

TWO 10-OUNCE PACKAGES FROZEN
     CAULIFLOWER FLORETS, THAWED

1 CUP HALF-AND-HALF

½ TEASPOON NUTMEG

¼ TEASPOON SALT

¼ TEASPOON BLACK PEPPER

½ CUP GRATED PARMESAN CHEESE

1. In a large skillet, cook the bacon over medium heat until crisp, about 10 minutes. Drain the bacon on paper towels; crumble and set aside. Drain off the bacon fat and wipe out the skillet with paper towels.

2. Add the oil to the skillet and warm over medium-high heat. Add the scallions and garlic, and cook, stirring frequently, until the garlic begins to brown, 2 to 3 minutes.

3. Meanwhile, in a large pot of boiling water, cook the pasta until al dente according to package directions.

4. Add the cauliflower to the skillet and cook, stirring constantly, until the cauliflower softens, 4 to 5 minutes.

5. Remove the skillet from the heat and, working directly in the skillet, use a potato masher to mash about half of the cauliflower. Stir in the half-and-half, nutmeg, salt, and pepper. Return the mixture to medium-high heat and simmer until slightly thickened, 3 to 4 minutes. Remove from the heat and stir in the Parmesan.

6. Drain the pasta and transfer it to a large serving bowl. Add the cauliflower sauce and the crumbled bacon, toss to combine, and serve hot.

PASTA RISOTTO WITH
YELLOW SQUASH AND RED PEPPER

SERVES 4

◇ LOW-FAT

3½ CUPS REDUCED-SODIUM CHICKEN
BROTH

2 TABLESPOONS UNSALTED BUTTER

2 GARLIC CLOVES, MINCED

1½ TEASPOONS OREGANO

½ TEASPOON BLACK PEPPER

PINCH OF RED PEPPER FLAKES

¾ POUND ORZO (ABOUT 2 CUPS)

1 SMALL YELLOW SQUASH, DICED

1 MEDIUM RED BELL PEPPER, DICED

1 CUP FROZEN PEAS

⅓ CUP GRATED PARMESAN CHEESE

¼ POUND HAM, PREFERABLY SMOKED,
CUT INTO 2-INCH MATCHSTICKS

¼ CUP CHOPPED PARSLEY

1. In a medium saucepan, bring the broth, butter, garlic, oregano, black pepper, and red pepper flakes to a boil over medium-high heat.

2. Add the orzo to the boiling broth, return to a boil, and cook, stirring frequently, for 3 minutes.

3. Stir in the squash, bell pepper, and peas, and return to a boil. Reduce the heat to low, cover, and simmer until the orzo and vegetables are tender, about 7 minutes.

4. Stir in the Parmesan, ham, and parsley until well combined, and serve.

KITCHEN NOTE: *In the classic Italian rice dish called risotto, rice is cooked slowly and stirred constantly to produce creamy, tender results. In this version, orzo (a rice-shaped pasta) is cooked in broth to produce a similar dish. The peas, ham, and Parmesan cheese used here are typical risotto components, as are the squash and pepper.*

PENNE WITH BELL PEPPERS, WHITE BEANS, AND THYME

SERVES 4

♦ EXTRA-QUICK

3 TABLESPOONS OLIVE OIL

1 MEDIUM RED ONION, THINLY SLICED

3 GARLIC CLOVES, MINCED

½ POUND PENNE OR OTHER MEDIUM, TUBULAR PASTA

1 LARGE GREEN BELL PEPPER, CUT INTO ½-INCH SQUARES

1 LARGE RED OR YELLOW BELL PEPPER, CUT INTO ½-INCH SQUARES

ONE 16-OUNCE CAN WHITE KIDNEY BEANS (CANNELLINI), RINSED AND DRAINED

2 TABLESPOONS FRESH LEMON JUICE

1 TEASPOON THYME

¾ TEASPOON SALT

¼ TEASPOON BLACK PEPPER

2 TABLESPOONS UNSALTED BUTTER

1. In a large skillet, warm 2 tablespoons of the oil over medium-high heat. Add the onion and garlic, and cook, stirring frequently, until the onion begins to brown, about 5 minutes.

2. Meanwhile, in a large pot of boiling water, cook the pasta until al dente according to package directions.

3. Add the remaining 1 tablespoon oil to the skillet. Add the bell peppers and cook, stirring frequently, until they begin to soften, about 5 minutes.

4. Stir in the white beans, lemon juice, thyme, salt, and black pepper. Cook, stirring frequently, until the beans are heated through, about 3 minutes. Remove from the heat.

5. Drain the pasta and transfer it to a large serving bowl. Add the butter and toss until melted. Add the vegetable mixture and toss gently to combine.

FETTUCCINE WITH BROILED EGGPLANT AND BASIL

SERVES 4

1 MEDIUM EGGPLANT, CUT LENGTHWISE INTO 1-INCH-THICK SLICES

2½ TABLESPOONS OIL FROM THE SUN-DRIED TOMATOES OR OLIVE OIL

½ POUND FETTUCCINE OR LINGUINE

1 LARGE FRESH TOMATO, HALVED AND SEEDED

½ CUP OIL-PACKED SUN-DRIED TOMATO HALVES, THINLY SLICED

2 TABLESPOONS MINCED SHALLOTS OR SCALLION WHITES

1 GARLIC CLOVE, MINCED

1 TABLESPOON RED WINE VINEGAR

BLACK PEPPER

¼ CUP CHOPPED FRESH BASIL

1. Preheat the broiler. Brush both sides of the eggplant slices with 1½ tablespoons of the oil. Cut each eggplant slice into 1-inch cubes. Place the eggplant cubes on a baking sheet in a single layer, then broil until well browned on one side. Turn the pieces over and broil until browned on the second side. Turn off the broiler, but leave the eggplant in the oven to keep it warm.

2. In a large pot of boiling water, cook the pasta until al dente according to package directions.

3. Meanwhile, in a food processor or blender, process the fresh tomato until puréed.

4. Transfer the tomato purée to a small saucepan. Stir in the sun-dried tomatoes, shallots, garlic, vinegar, the remaining 1 tablespoon oil, and a generous grinding of pepper. Bring the mixture to a simmer over low heat and cook, stirring frequently, for 2 minutes. Remove the pan from the heat and stir in the basil.

5. Drain the pasta and transfer to a large serving bowl. Add the warm eggplant cubes and the tomato sauce and toss to combine.

SPAGHETTI WITH PROVENÇAL SAUCE

SERVES 4

3 TABLESPOONS OLIVE OIL

½ MEDIUM EGGPLANT, PEELED AND
   CUT INTO ½-INCH CHUNKS

2 GARLIC CLOVES, PEELED

2 ANCHOVY FILLETS (OPTIONAL),
   RINSED AND COARSELY CHOPPED

1 CUP CANNED NO-SALT-ADDED WHOLE
   TOMATOES

2 LARGE RED OR YELLOW BELL
   PEPPERS, CUT INTO THIN STRIPS

2 TEASPOONS CAPERS, RINSED
   AND DRAINED

2 TEASPOONS CHOPPED FRESH BASIL,
   OR 1 TEASPOON DRIED

1 POUND SPAGHETTI

BLACK PEPPER

⅔ CUP GRATED ROMANO CHEESE

1. In a large nonstick skillet, warm the oil over medium heat. Add the eggplant, whole garlic cloves, and anchovies (if using). Cook, stirring occasionally, until the eggplant is soft, 5 to 8 minutes.

2. Stir in the tomatoes and break them up with the back of a spoon. Add the bell peppers, capers, and basil, and bring to a simmer. Cover and cook, stirring occasionally, until the peppers are tender, 12 to 15 minutes.

3. Meanwhile, in a large pot of boiling water, cook the pasta until al dente according to package directions.

4. Remove and discard the garlic cloves from the sauce. Stir a generous amount of black pepper into the sauce.

5. Drain the pasta and transfer it to a large serving bowl. Add the sauce and toss well to coat. Add ⅓ cup of the Romano and toss again. Pass the remaining cheese at the table.

Substitution: *Although the eggplant contributes significantly to the Provençal nature of this dish, zucchini can easily be substituted for those who do not like eggplant's slightly astringent taste. Cut the zucchini into ½-inch chunks and use about 2 cups.*

FLORENTINE-STYLE SAUTÉED RAVIOLI

SERVES 4

◆ EXTRA-QUICK

3 TABLESPOONS OLIVE OIL

1 MEDIUM ONION, THINLY SLICED

4 GARLIC CLOVES, MINCED

1 POUND CHEESE-FILLED RAVIOLI

½ POUND MUSHROOMS, THINLY SLICED

3 TABLESPOONS UNSALTED BUTTER

1½ TEASPOONS OREGANO

½ TEASPOON BLACK PEPPER

¼ TEASPOON SALT

1 POUND FRESH SPINACH, STEMMED,
OR TWO 10-OUNCE PACKAGES
FROZEN LEAF SPINACH, THAWED AND
SQUEEZED DRY

¼ CUP GRATED PARMESAN CHEESE

1. In a large skillet, warm 1 tablespoon of the oil over medium-high heat. Add the onion and garlic, and cook, stirring frequently, until the onion begins to soften, 2 to 3 minutes.

2. Meanwhile, in a large pot of boiling water, cook the ravioli until al dente according to package directions.

3. Add 1 tablespoon of the oil and the mushrooms to the skillet, and cook until they begin to soften, 3 to 5 minutes.

4. Add 2 tablespoons of the butter, the oregano, pepper, and salt. Stir in the spinach and cook until the spinach is just wilted and heated through, about 3 minutes.

5. Divide the spinach-mushroom mixture among 4 plates. Drain the ravioli. Warm the remaining 1 tablespoon oil with the remaining 1 tablespoon butter in the skillet until the butter is melted. Add the ravioli and stir-fry until they begin to brown, 2 to 3 minutes.

6. Spoon the ravioli on top of the spinach-mushroom mixture. Sprinkle with the Parmesan, and serve hot.

PASTA TWISTS WITH SPICY BROCCOLI SAUCE

SERVES 4

◆ EXTRA - QUICK

¾ POUND ROTINI OR OTHER SHORT
   PASTA TWISTS

2 TABLESPOONS OLIVE OIL

1 MEDIUM RED ONION, COARSELY
   CHOPPED

3 GARLIC CLOVES, MINCED

2 MEDIUM STALKS BROCCOLI, CUT
   INTO BITE-SIZE PIECES

1 LARGE RED BELL PEPPER, COARSELY
   CHOPPED

¾ TEASPOON OREGANO

½ TEASPOON SALT

¼ TEASPOON RED PEPPER FLAKES

¼ TEASPOON BLACK PEPPER

1 CUP HALF-AND-HALF

½ CUP GRATED PARMESAN CHEESE

1. In a large pot of boiling water, cook the pasta until al dente according to package directions.

2. Meanwhile, in a large skillet, warm 1 tablespoon of the oil over medium-high heat. Add the onion and garlic, and cook, stirring frequently, until the onion begins to brown, about 5 minutes.

3. Add the remaining 1 tablespoon oil to the skillet. Add the broccoli, bell pepper, oregano, salt, red pepper flakes, and black pepper, and stir-fry until the vegetables are crisp-tender, about 5 minutes.

4. Stir in the half-and-half and Parmesan until combined. Reduce the heat to medium, bring to a simmer, and cook, stirring constantly, until the mixture thickens slightly, 2 to 3 minutes. Remove from the heat.

5. Drain the pasta and transfer it to a large serving bowl. Add the broccoli sauce, toss to coat, and serve hot.

FETTUCCINE WITH GREEN VEGETABLES

SERVES 4

◆ EXTRA-QUICK

½ POUND FETTUCCINE OR OTHER
BROAD NOODLES

3 TABLESPOONS OLIVE OIL

3 TABLESPOONS UNSALTED BUTTER

8 SCALLIONS, COARSELY CHOPPED

5 GARLIC CLOVES, MINCED

ONE 10-OUNCE PACKAGE FROZEN
CHOPPED SPINACH, THAWED AND
SQUEEZED DRY

1 CUP FROZEN PEAS, THAWED

1 CUP FROZEN CHOPPED BROCCOLI,
THAWED AND DRAINED ON PAPER
TOWELS

¾ TEASPOON SALT

½ TEASPOON BLACK PEPPER

1¼ CUPS REDUCED-FAT SOUR CREAM

⅔ CUP GRATED PARMESAN CHEESE

1. In a large pot of boiling water, cook the pasta until al dente according to package directions.

2. Meanwhile, in a large skillet, warm the oil with the butter over medium heat until the butter is melted. Add the scallions and garlic, and cook until the scallions are wilted, about 5 minutes.

3. Increase the heat to medium-high and add the spinach, peas, broccoli, salt, and pepper. Cook, stirring frequently, until the vegetables are heated through, about 5 minutes.

4. Remove the skillet from the heat and stir in the sour cream until well combined.

5. Drain the pasta and transfer it to a large serving bowl. Add the vegetable mixture and the Parmesan, and toss well to combine.

Linguine and Broccoli with Peanut Sauce

SERVES 4

◆ EXTRA-QUICK

½ CUP PLUS 2 TABLESPOONS CREAMY
    PEANUT BUTTER
¼ CUP REDUCED-SODIUM SOY SAUCE
2 TABLESPOONS ORIENTAL (DARK)
    SESAME OIL
2 TEASPOONS DISTILLED WHITE
    VINEGAR
½ CUP CHICKEN BROTH
½ POUND LINGUINE OR SPAGHETTI

2 TABLESPOONS VEGETABLE OIL
3 GARLIC CLOVES, MINCED
2 MEDIUM STALKS BROCCOLI, CUT
    INTO BITE-SIZE PIECES
1 LARGE RED BELL PEPPER, CUT INTO
    BITE-SIZE PIECES
8 SCALLIONS, COARSELY CHOPPED
½ CUP (PACKED) CILANTRO SPRIGS

1. In a food processor or blender, combine the peanut butter, soy sauce, sesame oil, and vinegar, and process until blended. Gradually add the broth and process until smooth.

2. In a large pot of boiling water, cook the pasta until al dente according to package directions.

3. Meanwhile, in a large skillet, warm the vegetable oil over medium-high heat. Add the garlic and cook, stirring frequently, for 1 min-ute. Add the broccoli and bell pepper, and stir-fry until the vegetables are just tender, 5 to 8 minutes.

4. Stir in the scallions and cilantro, and remove the skillet from the heat.

5. Drain the pasta and transfer it to a large serving bowl. Add the peanut sauce and toss well to coat. Add the broccoli mixture, toss again, and serve.

Kitchen Note: *If you are counting fat grams, you can slim this recipe down by trying one of the reduced-fat peanut butters currently available in supermarkets. Just note that you may have to add some more broth or water to loosen up the sauce (Step 1), since the reduced-fat versions are much drier than their high-fat counterparts.*

Bow Ties in Red Pepper Sauce with Broccoli

SERVES 4

◆ EXTRA-QUICK   ◇ LOW-FAT

1 CUP BROCCOLI FLORETS

½ POUND BOW TIE PASTA OR OTHER
    FANCY PASTA SHAPE

1 TABLESPOON OLIVE OIL

1 GARLIC CLOVE, MINCED

2 MEDIUM RED BELL PEPPERS,
    COARSELY CHOPPED

¼ TEASPOON SALT

1 CUP CHICKEN BROTH, PREFERABLY
    REDUCED-SODIUM

¼ CUP GRATED PARMESAN CHEESE

1 TABLESPOON CHOPPED FRESH BASIL,
    OR 1 TEASPOON DRIED

½ TABLESPOON CHOPPED FRESH
    OREGANO, OR ½ TEASPOON DRIED

¼ TEASPOON BLACK PEPPER

1. In a large pot of boiling water, blanch the broccoli for 2 minutes. Reserve the boiling water for the pasta and, with a slotted spoon, transfer the broccoli to a colander. Drain, rinse under cold running water, and set aside.

2. In the same pot of boiling water, cook the pasta until al dente according to package directions.

3. Meanwhile, in a large nonstick skillet, warm the oil over medium heat. Add the garlic and cook, stirring frequently, until fragrant, about 30 seconds. Add the bell peppers and salt. Pour in the broth, bring to a simmer, and cook until the liquid is reduced to approximately ⅓ cup, about 7 minutes.

4. In a food processor or blender, process the bell pepper mixture until puréed. Strain the mixture through a sieve back into the skillet. Stir in the broccoli, Parmesan, basil, oregano, and black pepper. Simmer the sauce until the broccoli is heated through, 2 to 3 minutes.

5. Drain the pasta and transfer it to a large serving bowl. Add the broccoli-red pepper sauce, toss to coat, and serve.

PENNE WITH BROCCOLI ITALIANO

SERVES 4

◆ EXTRA - QUICK

1 POUND PENNE PASTA

1 POUND BROCCOLI RABE, HALVED
  CROSSWISE

2 TO 3 TABLESPOONS OLIVE OIL

2 GARLIC CLOVES, MINCED

½ CUP GRATED PARMESAN CHEESE

PINCH OF RED PEPPER FLAKES

1. In a large pot of boiling water, cook the pasta until al dente according to package directions. About 5 minutes before the pasta is done, add the broccoli rabe to the boiling water and cook until crisp-tender.

2. Meanwhile, in a small saucepan, warm the oil over medium heat. Add the garlic and cook, stirring frequently, until it is lightly browned, about 2 minutes. Remove from the heat.

3. Drain the pasta and broccoli rabe and transfer them to a large serving bowl. Add the garlic-oil mixture, the Parmesan, and red pepper flakes to taste, and toss to combine.

SUBSTITUTION: *Once considered a gourmet treat, broccoli rabe— also called rapini or broccoli rape—is now sold in some supermarkets. Despite its availability, many dislike its somewhat bitter taste; so to make this dish with regular broccoli instead, use the same amount (1 pound), but cut the broccoli lengthwise (including the florets) to make the stalks about the width of medium to medium- large asparagus.*

PASTA JAMBALAYA

SERVES 4

◇ LOW-FAT

1 TEASPOON OLIVE OIL

¼ POUND HOT ITALIAN SAUSAGE, CASINGS REMOVED

1 LARGE ONION, COARSELY CHOPPED

3 GARLIC CLOVES, MINCED

1 LARGE GREEN BELL PEPPER, COARSELY CHOPPED

1 LARGE RIB CELERY, COARSELY CHOPPED

ONE 14½-OUNCE CAN NO-SALT-ADDED WHOLE TOMATOES

½ TEASPOON SALT

¼ TEASPOON HOT PEPPER SAUCE

PINCH OF CAYENNE PEPPER

1 BAY LEAF

¾ POUND FUSILLI OR OTHER SHORT PASTA TWISTS

½ POUND SKINLESS, BONELESS CHICKEN BREASTS, CUT ACROSS THE GRAIN INTO ¼-INCH-WIDE STRIPS

1. In a large skillet, warm the oil over medium-high heat. Crumble in the sausage and cook until the sausage is no longer pink, 2 to 3 minutes.

2. Add the onion and garlic, and stir-fry until the onion begins to brown, about 5 minutes.

3. Add the bell pepper, celery, tomatoes, salt, hot pepper sauce, cayenne, and bay leaf, and bring to a boil, breaking up the tomatoes with the back of a spoon. Reduce the heat to low, cover, and simmer while you cook the pasta.

4. In a large pot of boiling water, cook the pasta until al dente according to package directions.

5. Uncover the sauce and bring it to a boil over medium-high heat. Add the chicken and cook, stirring frequently, until the chicken is just cooked through, about 5 minutes. Remove the skillet from the heat.

6. Drain the pasta and transfer it to a large serving bowl. Remove and discard the bay leaf from the sauce, spoon the sauce over the pasta, and toss to coat.

Spicy Chicken with Wagon Wheels

SERVES 4

◆ EXTRA-QUICK   ◇ LOW-FAT

3 CUPS CHICKEN BROTH, PREFERABLY
   REDUCED-SODIUM
1 CUP WATER
2 GARLIC CLOVES, MINCED
3 DROPS HOT PEPPER SAUCE
¼ TO ½ TEASPOON RED PEPPER FLAKES,
   TO TASTE
¼ TEASPOON BLACK PEPPER
2 LARGE SWEET POTATOES, PEELED AND
   CUT INTO ¼-INCH DICE

½ POUND WAGON WHEEL PASTA
1 LARGE GREEN BELL PEPPER, CUT INTO
   THIN STRIPS
½ POUND SKINLESS, BONELESS
   CHICKEN BREASTS, CUT ACROSS THE
   GRAIN INTO ¼-INCH-WIDE STRIPS
3 TABLESPOONS GRATED PARMESAN
   CHEESE

1. In a large skillet, combine the broth, water, garlic, hot pepper sauce, red pepper flakes, and black pepper, and bring to a boil over medium-high heat.

2. Add the sweet potatoes and the pasta to the boiling broth mixture. Stir well and return the mixture to a boil. Reduce the heat to medium-low, cover, and simmer until the pasta is al dente and the sweet potatoes are almost tender, about 7 minutes.

3. Return the pasta-sweet potato mixture to a boil over medium-high heat. Stir in the bell pepper and chicken, and return the mixture to a boil. Reduce the heat to medium-low, cover, and simmer, stirring occasionally, until the chicken is cooked through, about 5 minutes.

4. Remove the skillet from the heat and stir in the Parmesan. Serve hot.

Fettuccine with Chicken and Scallion-Cheese Sauce

SERVES 4

◆ EXTRA-QUICK

¼ CUP OLIVE OIL

8 SCALLIONS, COARSELY CHOPPED

2 GARLIC CLOVES, MINCED

1 TEASPOON OREGANO

½ POUND FETTUCCINE OR OTHER
BROAD NOODLES

1¼ POUNDS SKINLESS, BONELESS
CHICKEN BREASTS, CUT ACROSS THE
GRAIN INTO ¼-INCH-WIDE STRIPS

⅓ CUP PLUS 3 TABLESPOONS GRATED
PARMESAN CHEESE

½ TEASPOON SALT

¼ TEASPOON BLACK PEPPER

1 CUP LOW-FAT COTTAGE CHEESE

¼ CUP CHICKEN BROTH

1. In a large skillet, warm 2 tablespoons of the oil over medium heat. Add the scallions, garlic, and oregano, and stir-fry until the scallions are wilted, about 5 minutes. Transfer the mixture to a plate and set aside.

2. In a large pot of boiling water, cook the pasta until al dente according to package directions.

3. Meanwhile, add the remaining 2 tablespoons oil to the skillet and warm over medium-high heat. Add the chicken and stir-fry until lightly browned and cooked through,

3 to 4 minutes. Stir in the scallion mixture, 3 tablespoons of the Parmesan, the salt, and pepper. Remove from the heat.

4. In a small mixer bowl with an electric mixer, beat the cottage cheese until puréed. Stir in the broth and the remaining ⅓ cup of Parmesan.

5. Drain the pasta and add it to the chicken-scallion mixture in the skillet. Add the cottage cheese mixture, toss to combine, and serve.

Fusilli with Chicken and Rosemary Cream Sauce

SERVES 4

♦ EXTRA-QUICK

4 TABLESPOONS UNSALTED BUTTER

1 GARLIC CLOVE, CUT INTO QUARTERS

1 POUND SKINLESS, BONELESS CHICKEN
   BREASTS, CUT INTO ½-INCH
   SQUARES

1 CUP HALF-AND-HALF

1½ TEASPOONS CHOPPED FRESH
   ROSEMARY, OR ½ TEASPOON DRIED

1 CUP GRATED PARMESAN CHEESE

¼ TEASPOON SALT

¼ TEASPOON BLACK PEPPER

1 POUND FUSILLI OR OTHER SHORT
   PASTA TWISTS

½ CUP LOW-FAT MILK (OPTIONAL)

1. In a large skillet, warm the butter over medium heat until melted. Add the garlic and, with the back of a wooden spoon, press the garlic over the surface of the pan. Cook until the garlic is nut brown, then discard.

2. Increase the heat to high. Add the chicken and cook, stirring constantly, until browned and just cooked through, 1 to 2 minutes.

3. Add the half-and-half and rosemary, and bring to a simmer. Stir in ½ cup of the Parmesan and the salt and pepper. Remove from the heat and cover the pan.

4. In a large pot of boiling water, cook the pasta until al dente according to package directions.

5. Rewarm the sauce over medium heat. If the sauce is too thick, stir in some of the milk.

6. Drain the pasta and transfer it to a large serving bowl. Add the chicken and rosemary cream sauce, and toss well to combine. Pass the remaining Parmesan at the table.

Variation: *For a different herbal twist to this dish, try thyme or lemon thyme in place of the rosemary. The quantities should be approximately the same, although it would be safer to start with a small quantity and taste before adding more.*

ORIENTAL PASTA
WITH CHICKEN AND BROCCOLI

SERVES 4

2 BONE-IN CHICKEN BREAST HALVES

2 CUPS CHICKEN BROTH, PREFERABLY
REDUCED-SODIUM

3½ TABLESPOONS DRY SHERRY OR SAKE

1 TEASPOON ORIENTAL (DARK) SESAME
OIL

¼ TEASPOON SALT

PINCH OF WHITE PEPPER

¾ POUND VERMICELLI OR SPAGHETTINI

3 TABLESPOONS VEGETABLE OIL

2 CUPS SMALL BROCCOLI FLORETS

¼ TEASPOON SUGAR

½ TEASPOON SESAME SEEDS

2 FRESH JALAPEÑO PEPPERS, SEEDED
AND MINCED

1 TABLESPOON REDUCED-SODIUM
SOY SAUCE

4 SCALLIONS, FINELY CHOPPED

1. In a medium saucepan, place the chicken and enough water to cover. Bring to a boil, reduce the heat to low, and cook the chicken until just opaque, about 10 minutes. Transfer to a cutting board and discard the poaching liquid. Shred the meat and discard the bones and skin. Cover with foil.

2. Meanwhile, in a small saucepan, bring the broth to a boil over high heat. Add 2 tablespoons of the sherry, the sesame oil, salt, and white pepper. Reduce the heat to low and simmer the broth while you cook the pasta.

3. In a large pot of boiling water, cook the pasta until al dente according to package directions. Drain the pasta in a colander, rinse under cold running water, and set aside.

4. In a large skillet or wok, heat 1 tablespoon of the vegetable oil over medium-high heat. Add the broccoli and stir-fry until bright green. Add 1 tablespoon of the sherry and the sugar, and stir-fry for 30 seconds. Transfer the broccoli to a bowl, add the sesame seeds, and toss to blend. Cover with foil to keep warm.

5. Heat the remaining 2 tablespoons vegetable oil in the same skillet. Add the jalapeños and stir-fry for 30 seconds. Add the soy sauce and the remaining ½ tablespoon sherry. Add the chicken and scallions, and stir-fry for 1 minute.

6. Divide the pasta among 4 serving bowls and ladle the simmering broth on top. Place separate mounds of the chicken and broccoli mixtures over the pasta.

SPAGHETTI PRIMAVERA WITH CHICKEN

SERVES 4

◆ EXTRA-QUICK

½ POUND SPAGHETTI

5 TABLESPOONS LIGHT OLIVE OIL

¾ POUND SKINLESS, BONELESS
    CHICKEN BREASTS, CUT INTO
    1-INCH CUBES

½ POUND MUSHROOMS, THINLY SLICED

1 MEDIUM RED OR YELLOW BELL
    PEPPER, SLIVERED

8 SCALLIONS, COARSELY CHOPPED

2 GARLIC CLOVES, MINCED

¼ CUP CHOPPED FRESH DILL, OR
    1 TEASPOON DRIED

¾ TEASPOON SALT

¼ TEASPOON BLACK PEPPER

1. In a large pot of boiling water, cook the pasta until al dente according to package directions.

2. Meanwhile, in a large skillet or flameproof casserole, warm 2 tablespoons of the oil over medium-high heat. Add the chicken and cook, stirring frequently, until the chicken turns white, 2 to 3 minutes.

3. Add the mushrooms, bell pepper, scallions, garlic, and remaining 3 tablespoons oil, and cook, stirring frequently, until the vegetables are softened but not browned, 2 to 3 minutes.

4. Drain the pasta and add it to the skillet along with the dill, salt, and black pepper. Gently toss the ingredients to combine, and serve hot.

SWEET AFTERTHOUGHT: *Try this easy but elegant custard for dessert. Soak 4 ounces of dried apricots briefly in boiling water to soften them, then divide them among 4 custard cups arranged in a baking dish. Blend 1½ cups plain low-fat yogurt, 3 egg yolks, and 2 tablespoons sugar, and pour this mixture over the apricots. Pour boiling water into the baking dish to come halfway up the sides of the custard cups. Bake at 350° for 25 minutes, or until firm. Chill.*

Linguine and Chicken in Parsley Sauce

SERVES 4

◆ EXTRA-QUICK

1 TABLESPOON VEGETABLE OIL

2 TEASPOONS GRATED LEMON ZEST

1 TEASPOON MINCED FRESH GINGER

1 TEASPOON SUGAR

¼ TEASPOON SALT

1 CUP CHICKEN BROTH, PREFERABLY
  REDUCED-SODIUM

½ POUND LINGUINE

2 TABLESPOONS UNSALTED BUTTER

½ POUND SKINLESS, BONELESS
  CHICKEN BREASTS, CUT INTO
  ¾-INCH CUBES

2 SHALLOTS, FINELY CHOPPED

2 BUNCHES OF PARSLEY, STEMMED

1. In a small saucepan, heat the oil and lemon zest over medium heat for 4 minutes. Stir in the ginger, sugar, and salt, and cook, stirring frequently, until fragrant, about 3 minutes. Add the broth and bring to a boil. Cook until approximately ½ cup of the liquid remains, 5 to 7 minutes.

2. In a large pot of boiling water, cook the pasta until al dente according to package directions.

3. Meanwhile, in a large skillet, melt 1 tablespoon of the butter over medium-high heat. Add the chicken and shallots, and cook, stirring frequently, until the chicken is lightly browned and almost cooked through, about 3 minutes. Stir in the broth mixture and cook for 1 minute. Add the parsley and cook, stirring, for 3 minutes. Remove from the heat and stir in the remaining 1 tablespoon butter.

4. Drain the pasta and transfer it to a large serving bowl. Add the chicken and parsley sauce, and toss to combine. Cover and let stand, stirring once, for 5 minutes to meld the flavors.

Ziti with Chicken in Lemon-Cheese Sauce

SERVES 4

1½ cups low-fat cottage cheese

¼ cup reduced-fat sour cream

¼ cup grated Parmesan cheese

2 tablespoons fresh lemon juice

1 teaspoon grated lemon zest

1½ teaspoons dill

¼ teaspoon black pepper

3 tablespoons olive oil

1 medium onion, coarsely chopped

½ pound ziti or other medium, tubular pasta

1¼ pounds skinless, boneless chicken breasts, cut across the grain into ¼-inch-wide strips

1 medium yellow squash, thinly sliced

½ pound asparagus, cut into 2-inch lengths

⅓ cup chicken broth

1. In a food processor or blender, process the cottage cheese until smooth. Add the sour cream, Parmesan, lemon juice, lemon zest, dill, and pepper, and process until smooth. Set the lemon-cheese sauce aside.

2. In a large skillet, warm 2 tablespoons of the oil over medium-high heat. Add the onion and cook, stirring frequently, until it begins to brown, about 5 minutes.

3. Meanwhile, in a large pot of boiling water, cook the pasta until al dente according to package directions.

4. Add the remaining 1 tablespoon oil to the skillet and warm over medium-high heat. Add the chicken and cook, stirring frequently, until browned, about 3 minutes.

5. Stir in the squash, asparagus, and broth, and bring the mixture to a boil. Reduce the heat to medium-low, cover, and simmer until the vegetables are tender, about 5 minutes. Remove from the heat.

6. Drain the pasta and transfer it to a large serving bowl. Add the lemon-cheese sauce and toss to coat. Add the chicken-asparagus mixture, toss again, and serve at once.

PASTA WITH CHICKEN
in JALAPEÑO-TOMATO SAUCE

SERVES 4

2 TABLESPOONS OLIVE OIL

1 MEDIUM ONION, COARSELY CHOPPED

3 GARLIC CLOVES, MINCED

½ POUND SKINLESS, BONELESS
   CHICKEN BREASTS, CUT INTO
   BITE-SIZE PIECES

1 TABLESPOON UNSALTED BUTTER

1 TABLESPOON CUMIN

1½ TEASPOONS OREGANO

1 TABLESPOON FLOUR

ONE 28-OUNCE CAN CRUSHED
   TOMATOES

1 TABLESPOON NO-SALT-ADDED
   TOMATO PASTE

2 SMALL PICKLED JALAPEÑO PEPPERS,
   SEEDED AND MINCED

ONE 10-OUNCE PACKAGE FROZEN
   CORN KERNELS

¼ TEASPOON SALT

¼ TEASPOON BLACK PEPPER

¾ POUND SMALL PASTA SHELLS

¼ CUP MINCED CILANTRO

1. In a large skillet, warm 1 tablespoon of the oil over medium-high heat. Add the onion and garlic, and cook, stirring frequently, until the onion begins to brown, about 5 minutes.

2. Add the remaining 1 tablespoon oil and the chicken to the skillet, and stir-fry until the chicken is browned and cooked through, about 5 minutes. Transfer the chicken mixture to a bowl; cover to keep warm and set aside.

3. Add the butter to the skillet and warm until melted. Add the cumin and oregano, and stir-fry until fragrant, about 30 seconds. Stir in the flour and cook, stirring constantly, until the flour is no longer visible, about 30

seconds. Add the tomatoes, tomato paste, jalapeños, corn, salt, and pepper, and bring the mixture to a boil, stirring constantly. Reduce the heat to low, cover, and simmer while you cook the pasta.

4. In a large pot of boiling water, cook the pasta until al dente according to package directions.

5. Add the chicken mixture to the jalapeño-tomato sauce and stir to combine. Stir in the cilantro. Drain the pasta and transfer it to a large bowl. Spoon the sauce on top and serve hot.

SHELLS STUFFED WITH SMOKED TURKEY AND CHEESE

SERVES 4

2 CUPS NO-SALT-ADDED TOMATO
  SAUCE
ONE 15-OUNCE CONTAINER PART-SKIM
  RICOTTA CHEESE
¼ POUND PART-SKIM MOZZARELLA
  CHEESE, DICED
¼ CUP GRATED PARMESAN CHEESE
1 EGG, BEATEN

3 SLICES SMOKED TURKEY, FINELY
  CHOPPED
2 TEASPOONS CHOPPED FRESH BASIL
  OR PARSLEY
½ TEASPOON SALT
¼ TEASPOON BLACK PEPPER
PINCH OF NUTMEG
24 JUMBO PASTA SHELLS

1. Preheat the oven to 350°. Spoon a thin layer of tomato sauce over the bottom of a baking dish large enough to hold the pasta shells in a single layer.

2. In a medium bowl, combine the ricotta, mozzarella, and Parmesan. Beat in the egg and stir in the smoked turkey. Add the basil, salt, pepper, and nutmeg, and blend gently to mix.

3. Meanwhile, in a large pot of boiling water, cook the pasta shells until al dente according to package directions. Drain well in a colander, then rinse under cold water to prevent them from sticking. Shake the colander to remove any water caught in the shells.

4. Fill each shell with the ricotta mixture and arrange the shells, stuffed-side up, in the prepared baking dish.

5. Spoon the remaining tomato sauce over the shells and bake for 30 minutes, or until hot and bubbly.

SUBSTITUTION: *Any type of ham—baked, boiled, or smoked—could be used in place of the turkey. Other options are Canadian bacon or Italian prosciutto.*

Egg Noodles with Swiss Chicken Melt

SERVES 4 TO 6

2 TABLESPOONS OLIVE OIL

1 MEDIUM ONION, COARSELY CHOPPED

½ POUND SKINLESS, BONELESS
  CHICKEN BREASTS, CUT INTO
  BITE-SIZE PIECES

2 CUPS SHREDDED CABBAGE

¾ POUND WIDE EGG NOODLES

3 TABLESPOONS UNSALTED BUTTER

3 TABLESPOONS FLOUR

1 CUP CHICKEN BROTH, PREFERABLY
  REDUCED-SODIUM

1 CUP REDUCED-FAT SOUR CREAM

1 TABLESPOON DIJON MUSTARD

1½ TEASPOONS TARRAGON

¼ TEASPOON BLACK PEPPER

1½ CUPS SHREDDED SWISS CHEESE

½ CUP GRATED PARMESAN CHEESE

1. In a large broilerproof skillet, warm 1 tablespoon of the oil over medium-high heat. Add the onion and cook, stirring frequently, until the onion begins to brown, 3 to 4 minutes.

2. Add the remaining 1 tablespoon oil to the pan. Add the chicken and stir-fry until it is opaque and almost cooked through, 2 to 3 minutes.

3. Add the cabbage and cook, stirring frequently, until the cabbage is just wilted, about 4 minutes. Transfer the chicken mixture to a plate and cover loosely to keep warm. Set the skillet aside.

4. In a large pot of boiling water, cook the noodles until al dente according to package directions.

5. Meanwhile, preheat the broiler. In the same skillet, melt the butter over medium-high heat. Stir in the flour and cook, stirring constantly, until the flour is no longer visible, about 1 minute. Stir in the broth, sour cream, mustard, tarragon, and pepper. Bring to a boil, stirring constantly, and cook until the mixture is slightly thickened. Remove the skillet from the heat.

6. Drain the noodles and add them to the sauce in the skillet. Stir in the chicken mixture, 1 cup of the Swiss cheese, and ¼ cup of the Parmesan. Sprinkle the remaining ½ cup Swiss cheese and the remaining ¼ cup Parmesan on top and broil 4 inches from the heat for 3 to 5 minutes, or until the top is golden.

Pasta Twists with Turkey and Garlic-Pepper Cream

SERVES 4

½ CUP CHICKEN BROTH

3 MEDIUM CARROTS, CUT INTO 2-INCH MATCHSTICKS

3 GARLIC CLOVES, PEELED

½ POUND ROTINI OR OTHER SHORT PASTA TWISTS

ONE 8-OUNCE PACKAGE NEUFCHÂTEL CREAM CHEESE

2 TABLESPOONS GRATED PARMESAN CHEESE

½ TEASPOON BLACK PEPPER

½ TEASPOON SALT

2 TABLESPOONS MILK

1½ CUPS CUBED ROAST TURKEY (ABOUT ½ POUND)

8 SCALLIONS, COARSELY CHOPPED

1. In a medium saucepan, bring the broth to a boil over medium-high heat. Add the carrots and garlic. Reduce the heat to medium-low, cover, and simmer for 5 minutes. Drain the carrots and garlic, reserving the broth. Set the garlic and carrots aside.

2. Meanwhile, in a large pot of boiling water, cook the pasta until al dente according to package directions.

3. In a food processor or blender, process the garlic until minced. Add the cream cheese, Parmesan, pepper, salt, and reserved broth, and process until well combined. With the machine running, add the milk and process until smooth.

4. Drain the pasta and transfer it to a large serving bowl. While the pasta is still hot, add the cream cheese mixture, carrots, turkey, and scallions, and toss well to combine. Serve hot.

KITCHEN NOTE: *You could also make this dish with cooked chicken, which, though not as available as roast turkey is at deli counters, is very quickly cooked from scratch in the microwave. Place about ¾ pound of skinless, boneless chicken breast in a shallow microwave-safe dish, cover loosely, and cook at High for about 4½ minutes, or until the chicken is cooked through.*

Mexican-Style Pasta with Turkey and Vegetables

SERVES 4

◇ LOW-FAT

4 CUPS REDUCED-SODIUM CHICKEN
  BROTH
1 GARLIC CLOVE, MINCED
1 TEASPOON CUMIN
½ TEASPOON CHILI POWDER
½ POUND SKINLESS, BONELESS TURKEY
  BREAST
1 TABLESPOON VEGETABLE OIL
¾ POUND VERMICELLI OR
  SPAGHETTINI, BROKEN INTO
  2-INCH PIECES

6 CANNED NO-SALT-ADDED WHOLE
  TOMATOES, WELL DRAINED AND
  CHOPPED
3 SCALLIONS, COARSELY CHOPPED
1 LARGE GREEN BELL PEPPER, COARSELY
  CHOPPED
ONE 4-OUNCE CAN CHOPPED MILD
  GREEN CHILIES, DRAINED
¼ TEASPOON SALT
¼ CUP MINCED CILANTRO

1. In a medium saucepan, bring the broth, garlic, cumin, and chili powder to a boil over medium-high heat.

2. Add the turkey to the boiling broth, reduce the heat to medium-low, cover, and simmer until the turkey is cooked through, about 10 minutes. With a slotted spoon, transfer the turkey to a cutting board and set aside to cool. Reserve the broth mixture.

3. In a large nonstick skillet, warm the oil over medium-high heat. Add the pasta and cook, stirring constantly, until the pasta is lightly browned, about 2 minutes.

4. Add the broth mixture, tomatoes, scallions, bell pepper, green chilies, and salt, and bring the mixture to a boil over medium-high heat. Reduce the heat to low, cover, and simmer, stirring occasionally, until the pasta is al dente, about 7 minutes.

5. Meanwhile, shred the turkey.

6. Stir the shredded turkey and cilantro into the pasta mixture, and serve at once.

Spaghetti with Ground Turkey-Tomato Sauce

SERVES 4

◇ L O W - F A T

½ POUND GROUND TURKEY

6 GARLIC CLOVES—3 MINCED AND
   3 LIGHTLY CRUSHED

1½ TEASPOONS OREGANO

¾ TEASPOON SALT

½ TEASPOON BLACK PEPPER

1 TABLESPOON OLIVE OIL

1 MEDIUM ONION, COARSELY CHOPPED

ONE 35-OUNCE CAN NO-SALT-ADDED
   WHOLE TOMATOES

2 TABLESPOONS TOMATO PASTE

1 BAY LEAF

½ POUND WHOLE WHEAT SPAGHETTI
   OR REGULAR SPAGHETTI

1. In a medium bowl, combine the turkey, minced garlic, ½ teaspoon of the oregano, ½ teaspoon of the salt, and ¼ teaspoon of the pepper. Mix lightly to combine.

2. In a medium saucepan, warm the oil over medium-high heat. Add the turkey mixture, the crushed whole garlic, and the onion, and cook, stirring frequently to break up the mixture, until the turkey turns white and just begins to brown, 3 to 5 minutes.

3. Add the tomatoes, breaking them up with the back of a spoon. Stir in the tomato paste, bay leaf, and the remaining 1 teaspoon oregano, ¼ teaspoon salt, and ¼ teaspoon pepper.

Bring the mixture to a boil, reduce the heat to medium-low, and simmer, stirring occasionally, until the sauce is slightly thickened, about 20 minutes.

4. Meanwhile, in a large pot of boiling water, cook the pasta until al dente according to package directions.

5. Remove and discard the bay leaf and the crushed garlic cloves from the sauce. Drain the pasta and divide it among 4 serving plates. Spoon the turkey-tomato sauce on top of the pasta and serve hot.

EGG NOODLES WITH CHILI-SPICED TURKEY

SERVES 4

1 CUP PLAIN LOW-FAT YOGURT
1 TABLESPOON VEGETABLE OIL
1 MEDIUM ONION, FINELY CHOPPED
1 POUND GROUND TURKEY
2½ TEASPOONS CHILI POWDER
½ TEASPOON SALT

½ POUND WIDE CURLY EGG NOODLES
1 MEDIUM TOMATO, CHOPPED
¼ CUP CHOPPED FRESH MINT, OR
  2 TABLESPOONS DRIED
1 TABLESPOON FRESH LEMON JUICE
1 TABLESPOON UNSALTED BUTTER

1. Spoon the yogurt into a fine-mesh sieve or a cheesecloth-lined sieve set over a bowl and set aside to drain for at least 20 minutes.

2. Meanwhile, in a large nonstick skillet, warm the oil over medium-high heat. Add the onion and stir-fry until softened, about 3 minutes. Add the turkey, 2 teaspoons of the chili powder, and the salt, and cook, stirring frequently to break up the turkey, until the turkey is browned and just cooked through, about 5 minutes. Stir in the tomato and cook for 2 minutes. Remove from the heat.

3. In a large pot of boiling water, cook the noodles until al dente according to package directions.

4. Discard the yogurt whey and transfer the drained yogurt to the bowl. Stir in 3 tablespoons of the fresh mint (or 1½ tablespoons dried), the lemon juice, and the remaining ½ teaspoon chili powder.

5. Drain the noodles and return them to the pasta cooking pot. Add the butter and toss gently until the noodles are coated.

6. Divide the hot noodles among 4 serving plates. Spoon the turkey mixture on top. Spoon the yogurt sauce over the turkey and noodles, sprinkle the remaining mint over the top, and serve hot.

SKILLET MACARONI WITH TURKEY AND ZUCCHINI

SERVES 4

◆ EXTRA-QUICK

1 TABLESPOON OLIVE OIL

1 MEDIUM ONION, COARSELY CHOPPED

2 GARLIC CLOVES, MINCED

½ POUND GROUND TURKEY

½ POUND SMALL ELBOW MACARONI

ONE 18-OUNCE CAN REDUCED-SODIUM TOMATO JUICE

1 CUP CHICKEN BROTH, PREFERABLY REDUCED-SODIUM

½ TEASPOON OREGANO

⅛ TEASPOON BLACK PEPPER

2 SMALL ZUCCHINI, HALVED LENGTHWISE AND CUT CROSSWISE INTO THIN HALF-ROUNDS

1. In a large skillet, warm the oil over medium-high heat. Add the onion and garlic, and cook, stirring frequently, until the onion is translucent, 2 to 3 minutes.

2. Add the turkey and cook, stirring to break up the meat, until the turkey is no longer pink, about 5 minutes.

3. Add the pasta, tomato juice, broth, oregano, and pepper, and bring to a boil. Cover, reduce the heat to medium-low, and simmer, stirring occasionally, for 10 minutes.

4. Stir in the zucchini and cook until the pasta and zucchini are tender, about 3 minutes. Serve hot.

SWEET AFTERTHOUGHT: *When pineapples are available, try this quick dessert. Peel and core a ripe pineapple and cut the flesh into chunks. Add 2 small bananas cut into slices and toss together. Add ¼ cup chopped toasted walnuts and a splash of dark rum or bourbon. If the pineapple is not very sweet, sprinkle the fruit with a little bit of brown sugar.*

Macaroni with Turkey Chili

SERVES 4

◆ EXTRA - QUICK ◇ LOW - FAT

¼ CUP CHICKEN BROTH

1 TABLESPOON CORNSTARCH

ONE 14½-OUNCE CAN NO-SALT-ADDED
   WHOLE TOMATOES

1 LARGE GREEN BELL PEPPER, DICED

1 MEDIUM ONION, COARSELY CHOPPED

4 GARLIC CLOVES, MINCED

½ POUND GROUND TURKEY

3 TABLESPOONS CHILI POWDER

2 TABLESPOONS TOMATO PASTE

¼ TEASPOON BLACK PEPPER

½ POUND SMALL ELBOW MACARONI

1 CUP CANNED RED KIDNEY BEANS,
   RINSED AND DRAINED

⅓ CUP GRATED CHEDDAR CHEESE

1. In a small bowl, combine the broth and cornstarch. Stir to blend and set aside.

2. In a medium saucepan, combine the tomatoes, bell pepper, onion, garlic, turkey, chili powder, tomato paste, and black pepper. Bring to a boil over medium-high heat, breaking up the tomatoes and the turkey with the back of a spoon. Reduce the heat to low, cover, and simmer, stirring occasionally, while you cook the pasta.

3. In a large pot of boiling water, cook the pasta until al dente according to package directions.

4. Just before the pasta is done, bring the chili to a boil over medium-high heat. Stir in the cornstarch mixture and the kidney beans, and cook, stirring constantly, until the mixture thickens and the beans are heated through, 1 to 2 minutes. Remove the saucepan from the heat.

5. Drain the pasta and transfer it to a large bowl. Add the turkey chili and toss to combine. Divide the mixture among 4 serving bowls and sprinkle some Cheddar on top of each.

Substitution: *Instead of red kidney beans you can use almost any canned bean, such as white kidney beans (also called cannellini), pinto beans, or black beans.*

Wagon Wheels with Sausage Sauce

SERVES 4

◇ LOW-FAT

2 TABLESPOONS OLIVE OIL

4 GARLIC CLOVES, MINCED

1 MEDIUM ONION, COARSELY CHOPPED

¾ POUND GROUND TURKEY

1 TABLESPOON RED WINE VINEGAR

1 TEASPOON FENNEL SEEDS

1 TEASPOON OREGANO

¼ TEASPOON RED PEPPER FLAKES

1 LARGE RIB CELERY, COARSELY CHOPPED

1 MEDIUM GREEN BELL PEPPER, COARSELY CHOPPED

½ POUND MUSHROOMS, COARSELY CHOPPED

ONE 14½-OUNCE CAN NO-SALT-ADDED WHOLE TOMATOES

ONE 8-OUNCE CAN TOMATO SAUCE

2 TABLESPOONS TOMATO PASTE

1 TEASPOON SUGAR

½ TEASPOON SALT

¾ POUND WAGON WHEEL PASTA

¼ CUP GRATED PARMESAN CHEESE

1. In a large saucepan, warm the oil over medium-high heat. Add the garlic and onion, and cook, stirring frequently, until the onion begins to brown, about 5 minutes.

2. Crumble in the ground turkey and cook, stirring frequently to break it up, until the turkey is no longer pink, about 3 minutes. Add the vinegar, fennel seeds, oregano, and red pepper flakes, and cook, stirring frequently, until fragrant, about 30 seconds.

3. Add the celery, bell pepper, mushrooms, and tomatoes; break up the tomatoes with the back of a spoon. Stir in the tomato sauce, tomato paste, sugar, and salt, and bring the mixture to a boil. Reduce the heat to medium-low and simmer, stirring frequently, for 15 minutes.

4. Meanwhile, in a large pot of boiling water, cook the pasta until al dente according to package directions.

5. Drain the pasta and divide it among 4 shallow bowls. Spoon the turkey sauce on top and sprinkle with the Parmesan.

Mock Lasagna with Turkey Sausage

SERVES 4

1 TABLESPOON OLIVE OIL

½ POUND COUNTRY-STYLE TURKEY
  SAUSAGE, CASINGS REMOVED

1 MEDIUM ONION, COARSELY CHOPPED

3 GARLIC CLOVES, MINCED

½ POUND BOW TIE PASTA OR OTHER
  FANCY PASTA SHAPE

ONE 15-OUNCE CAN TOMATO PURÉE

2 TABLESPOONS TOMATO PASTE

1 BAY LEAF

1½ TEASPOONS BASIL

½ TEASPOON RED PEPPER FLAKES

½ TEASPOON SALT

¼ TEASPOON BLACK PEPPER

2 CUPS SHREDDED PART-SKIM
  MOZZARELLA CHEESE

1. In a large nonstick skillet, warm the oil over medium heat. Crumble in the turkey sausage and cook, stirring frequently to break it up, until the sausage is browned, about 5 minutes. Add the onion and garlic, and cook, stirring frequently, until the onion is translucent, 3 to 4 minutes.

2. In a large pot of boiling water, cook the pasta until al dente according to package directions.

3. Meanwhile, add the tomato purée, tomato paste, bay leaf, basil, red pepper flakes, salt, and black pepper to the skillet. Stir well to combine, increase the heat to medium-high,

and bring the mixture to a boil. Reduce the heat to low, cover, and simmer the tomato sauce for 10 minutes.

4. Preheat the oven to 400°. Drain the pasta. Remove the tomato sauce from the heat. Remove and discard the bay leaf from the sauce.

5. Cover the bottom of an 8-inch square baking dish with one-third of the sauce. Top with half the pasta and sprinkle with half the mozzarella. Add half the remaining sauce, then all the remaining pasta. Top with the remaining sauce and mozzarella.

6. Bake for 15 minutes, or until the mock lasagna is heated through.

COUNTRY-STYLE RIGATONI WITH SMOKED TURKEY

SERVES 4

2 TABLESPOONS OLIVE OIL

2 TABLESPOONS UNSALTED BUTTER

1 MEDIUM ONION, THINLY SLICED

¼ POUND SMOKED TURKEY, CUT INTO SMALL CUBES

½ CUP THINLY SLICED MUSHROOMS

¼ TEASPOON BLACK PEPPER

½ POUND RIGATONI PASTA

2 LARGE RED POTATOES, CUT INTO ¼-INCH DICE

1 MEDIUM BUNCH BROCCOLI, CUT INTO FLORETS

½ CUP DRY WHITE WINE OR REDUCED-SODIUM CHICKEN BROTH

½ TEASPOON OREGANO

2 TABLESPOONS CHOPPED PARSLEY

½ CUP GRATED PARMESAN CHEESE

1. In a medium skillet, warm the oil with the butter over medium-high heat until the butter is melted. Add the onion and cook, stirring frequently, until softened, about 5 minutes. Add the turkey, mushrooms, and pepper, and cook, stirring, until the mushrooms start to give up their liquid, 3 to 4 minutes.

2. In a large pot of boiling water, cook the pasta until al dente according to package directions. During the last 8 minutes of cooking, add the potatoes and broccoli to the boiling water and cook until tender.

3. Meanwhile, add the wine, oregano, and 1 tablespoon of the parsley to the turkey mixture. Bring to a boil, reduce the heat to low, cover, and simmer while the pasta and vegetables are cooking.

4. Drain the pasta and vegetables and transfer them to a large serving bowl. Add the turkey mixture and toss well to combine. Add the Parmesan and the remaining 1 tablespoon parsley and toss again. Serve hot.

Bow Ties with Smoked Turkey and Spinach Sauce

SERVES 4

1 TABLESPOON OLIVE OIL

1 TABLESPOON UNSALTED BUTTER

4 SHALLOTS OR 1 SMALL ONION,
COARSELY CHOPPED

2 GARLIC CLOVES, MINCED

½ POUND BOW TIE PASTA OR OTHER
FANCY PASTA SHAPE

1 CUP HALF-AND-HALF

½ CUP DRY WHITE WINE OR REDUCED-
SODIUM CHICKEN BROTH

½ CUP REDUCED-SODIUM CHICKEN
BROTH

½ TEASPOON NUTMEG

¼ TEASPOON BLACK PEPPER

ONE 10-OUNCE PACKAGE FROZEN
CHOPPED SPINACH, THAWED AND
SQUEEZED DRY

½ POUND SMOKED TURKEY, CUT INTO
MATCHSTICKS

1. In a large skillet, warm the oil with the butter over medium heat until the butter is melted. Add the shallots and garlic, and cook, stirring frequently, until the shallots begin to brown, about 5 minutes.

2. In a large pot of boiling water, cook the pasta until al dente according to package directions.

3. Meanwhile, add the half-and-half, wine, broth, nutmeg, and pepper to the skillet. Bring the mixture to a boil, reduce the heat to low, and simmer for 5 minutes, stirring occasionally.

4. Increase the heat to medium-high and bring the sauce to a boil. Stir in the spinach, return the sauce to a boil, and reduce the heat to low. Cover and simmer, stirring occasionally, until the spinach is heated through, about 3 minutes. Remove from the heat.

5. Drain the pasta and transfer it to a large serving bowl. Add the spinach sauce and the turkey, and toss well to combine.

GREEK-STYLE PASTA
WITH SHRIMP AND FETA

SERVES 6

◇ L O W - F A T

2 TABLESPOONS OLIVE OIL

1 MEDIUM ONION, THINLY SLICED

3 GARLIC CLOVES, MINCED

2 CUPS CANNED NO-SALT-ADDED
WHOLE TOMATOES IN TOMATO
PURÉE

1 TEASPOON OREGANO

½ TEASPOON BASIL

¼ TEASPOON BLACK PEPPER

¾ POUND FETTUCCINE

¾ POUND MEDIUM SHRIMP, SHELLED
AND DEVEINED

½ CUP PITTED SLICED BLACK OLIVES

¼ POUND FETA CHEESE, CRUMBLED

1. In a large skillet, warm the oil over medium-high heat. Add the onion and garlic, and cook, stirring frequently, until the mixture begins to brown, about 5 minutes.

2. Stir in the tomatoes, breaking them up with the back of a spoon. Stir in the oregano, basil, and pepper, and bring the mixture to a boil. Reduce the heat to low, cover, and simmer, stirring occasionally, while you cook the pasta.

3. In a large pot of boiling water, cook the pasta until al dente according to package directions.

4. Uncover the tomato sauce, increase the heat to medium-high, and bring the sauce to a boil. Add the shrimp, reduce the heat to low, cover, and simmer until the shrimp are just cooked through, about 3 minutes. Add the olives and half of the feta cheese, and stir to combine. Remove from the heat.

5. Drain the pasta and transfer it to a large bowl. Spoon the shrimp mixture on top and toss to combine. Divide the mixture among 6 shallow bowls and crumble the remaining feta cheese on top.

SWEET AFTERTHOUGHT: *For a simple dessert in keeping with this Greek-style main course, serve scoops of ice cream topped with honey and finely chopped pistachio nuts. If you have the time, warm the honey first for a tastier treat.*

FETTUCCINE WITH CARIBBEAN SHRIMP SAUCE

SERVES 6

◇ LOW-FAT

¾ POUND FETTUCCINE, HALF SPINACH
AND HALF REGULAR

1 TABLESPOON OLIVE OIL

2 MEDIUM ONIONS, THINLY SLICED

3 GARLIC CLOVES, MINCED

2 TABLESPOONS CURRY POWDER

5 CANNED NO-SALT-ADDED WHOLE
TOMATOES

1 LARGE GREEN BELL PEPPER, DICED

1 CUP CANNED TOMATO PURÉE

¾ POUND MEDIUM SHRIMP, SHELLED
AND DEVEINED

2 TABLESPOONS FRESH LIME JUICE

2 TEASPOONS GRATED LIME ZEST

½ TEASPOON SUGAR

½ TEASPOON SALT

½ TEASPOON BLACK PEPPER

¼ TEASPOON RED PEPPER FLAKES

1 TABLESPOON UNSALTED BUTTER

1. In a large pot of boiling water, cook the pasta until al dente according to package directions.

2. Meanwhile, in a large skillet, warm the oil over medium-high heat. Add the onions and garlic, and cook, stirring frequently, until the onions begin to brown, about 3 minutes. Add the curry powder and cook, stirring constantly, until the curry powder is fragrant, about 1 minute.

3. Add the tomatoes, breaking them up with the back of a spoon. Stir in the bell pepper and the tomato purée, and bring the mixture to a boil.

4. Stir in the shrimp, lime juice, lime zest, sugar, salt, black pepper, and red pepper flakes, and return the mixture to a boil. Reduce the heat to low, cover, and simmer until the shrimp are just cooked through, about 4 minutes. Remove the pan from the heat and swirl in the butter.

5. Drain the pasta and transfer it to a large serving bowl. Add the shrimp sauce, toss well to combine, and serve hot.

Pasta Twists with Shrimp, Peas, and Tomato

SERVES 4

1 TABLESPOON OLIVE OIL

1 MEDIUM ONION, COARSELY CHOPPED

3 GARLIC CLOVES, MINCED

½ POUND ROTINI OR OTHER SHORT
 PASTA TWISTS

2 MEDIUM TOMATOES, COARSELY
 CHOPPED

⅓ CUP DRY WHITE WINE OR CHICKEN
 BROTH

¾ TEASPOON BASIL

½ TEASPOON SALT

¼ TEASPOON BLACK PEPPER

¾ POUND MEDIUM SHRIMP, SHELLED
 AND DEVEINED

1 CUP FROZEN PEAS

2 TABLESPOONS UNSALTED BUTTER

1. In a large skillet, warm the oil over medium-high heat. Add the onion and garlic, and cook, stirring frequently, until the onion begins to brown, about 5 minutes.

2. In a large pot of boiling water, cook the pasta until al dente according to package directions.

3. Meanwhile, add the tomatoes, wine, basil, salt, and pepper to the skillet. Bring the mixture to a boil over medium-high heat. Reduce the heat to medium-low, cover, and simmer for 10 minutes.

4. Increase the heat under the skillet to medium-high and return the tomato mixture to a boil. Add the shrimp and peas, return to a boil, and reduce the heat to medium-low. Cover and simmer, stirring occasionally, until the shrimp are cooked through, about 5 minutes. Remove from the heat and swirl in the butter.

5. Drain the pasta and transfer it to a large serving bowl. Add the shrimp and tomato sauce, toss well to combine, and serve hot.

SPAGHETTI WITH SHRIMP AND MUSHROOMS

SERVES 4

½ POUND SPAGHETTI

½ CUP HALF-AND-HALF

½ CUP GRATED PARMESAN CHEESE

¼ CUP CHOPPED PARSLEY

4 TEASPOONS ANCHOVY PASTE
(OPTIONAL)

½ TEASPOON DRY MUSTARD

¼ TEASPOON BLACK PEPPER

3 TABLESPOONS OLIVE OIL

¼ POUND MUSHROOMS, THINLY SLICED

2 GARLIC CLOVES, MINCED

¾ POUND MEDIUM SHRIMP, SHELLED
AND DEVEINED

8 SCALLIONS, COARSELY CHOPPED

1. In a large pot of boiling water, cook the pasta until al dente according to package directions.

2. Meanwhile, in a large serving bowl, combine the half-and-half, Parmesan, parsley, anchovy paste (if using), mustard, and pepper. Stir to mix and set aside.

3. In a large skillet, warm 2 tablespoons of the oil over medium-high heat. Add the mushrooms and garlic, and stir-fry until the mushrooms are softened, about 5 minutes.

4. Add the remaining 1 tablespoon oil and the shrimp to the skillet and stir-fry for 2 minutes. Add the scallions and stir-fry until the shrimp are just opaque, 1 to 2 minutes. Remove from the heat.

5. Drain the pasta. Add the hot pasta to the half-and-half mixture and toss to coat. Add the shrimp-vegetable mixture and toss to combine. Serve hot.

KITCHEN NOTE: *To save on preparation time, try using jumbo shrimp instead of medium shrimp: There will be fewer shrimp to shell. Although jumbo shrimp cost more, you can actually get away with buying less than 1 pound since the proportion of meat to shell is greater with the larger shrimp.*

VERMICELLI WITH SHRIMP AND BUTTERY BREAD CRUMBS

SERVES 4

⅔ POUND MEDIUM SHRIMP, SHELLED,
  DEVEINED, AND HALVED
  LENGTHWISE

4 SHALLOTS OR 1 SMALL ONION,
  COARSELY CHOPPED

2 GARLIC CLOVES, MINCED

½ TEASPOON FENNEL SEEDS
  (OPTIONAL), CRUSHED

¼ TEASPOON BLACK PEPPER

2 TABLESPOONS OLIVE OIL

1 LEMON, HALVED

2 MEDIUM FENNEL BULBS (ABOUT ⅔
  POUND)

3 TABLESPOONS UNSALTED BUTTER

¼ CUP UNSEASONED DRY BREAD
  CRUMBS

¾ POUND VERMICELLI OR SPAGHETTINI

1. In a large bowl, combine the shrimp, shallots, garlic, fennel seeds (if using), and pepper. Add 1 tablespoon of the oil and mix well. Squeeze the juice of one lemon half over the shrimp mixture, mix well, and set aside.

2. Trim the stalks and feathery tops from the fennel bulbs and discard (or save for another use). Cut the bulbs crosswise into very thin slices. Place the sliced fennel in a small bowl and squeeze the juice of the remaining lemon half over the fennel.

3. In a large skillet, heat the remaining 1 tablespoon oil over high heat. Add the fennel and cook, stirring constantly, for 5 minutes. Add the shrimp mixture and cook just until the shrimp turn pink, about 2 minutes. With a slotted spoon, transfer the shrimp and fennel to a large serving bowl and set aside.

4. Reduce the heat under the skillet to low. Add the butter and warm until melted. Add the bread crumbs and cook, stirring frequently, until crisp and golden brown, about 4 minutes. Remove from the heat.

5. Meanwhile, in a large pot of boiling water, cook the pasta until al dente according to package directions. Drain the pasta, add it to the shrimp-fennel mixture, and toss to combine. Scatter the bread crumbs over the pasta and serve hot.

PASTA AND MUSSELS WITH TOMATO-GARLIC SAUCE

SERVES 4

1 POUND MUSSELS, SCRUBBED AND
   DEBEARDED
½ CUP WATER
½ CUP DRY WHITE WINE OR REDUCED-
   SODIUM CHICKEN BROTH
¼ CUP OLIVE OIL
2 GARLIC CLOVES, FINELY MINCED
2 LARGE TOMATOES, COARSELY
   CHOPPED
3 TABLESPOONS TOMATO PASTE

½ POUND ZITI OR OTHER MEDIUM,
   TUBULAR PASTA
¼ CUP CHOPPED PARSLEY
1 TEASPOON BASIL
¼ TEASPOON OREGANO
¼ TEASPOON SALT
¼ TEASPOON BLACK PEPPER
⅛ TEASPOON THYME
⅛ TEASPOON SAGE

1. In a large saucepan, combine the mussels, water, and wine; cover and bring to a boil, and continue to cook until the mussels open. Transfer the mussels to a bowl to cool, discarding any mussels that do not open. Pour the mussel cooking liquid through a strainer lined with a paper towel or coffee filter; set the mussel broth aside.

2. In a large skillet, warm the oil over low heat. Add the garlic and cook until fragrant, about 1 minute. Add the tomatoes, strained mussel broth, and tomato paste. Stir in any liquid that has accumulated in the bowl with the mussels. Increase the heat to medium and cook until the mixture is thickened, 12 to 15 minutes.

3. Meanwhile remove the mussels from the shells and discard the shells.

4. In a large pot of boiling water, cook the pasta until al dente according to package directions.

5. Reduce the heat under the skillet to low. Stir the parsley, basil, oregano, salt, pepper, thyme, and sage into the tomato sauce.

6. Drain the pasta, add it to the skillet, and heat for 1 minute. Add the mussels and mix thoroughly. Divide the mixture among 4 shallow soup bowls and serve hot.

Linguine with Spicy Parsley-Clam Sauce

SERVES 4

◆ EXTRA-QUICK

2 TABLESPOONS OLIVE OIL

2 TABLESPOONS UNSALTED BUTTER

1 MEDIUM RED ONION, THINLY SLICED

4 GARLIC CLOVES, MINCED

½ POUND LINGUINE

2 TABLESPOONS FLOUR

1 CUP CHICKEN BROTH, PREFERABLY
   REDUCED-SODIUM

½ TO 1 TEASPOON RED PEPPER FLAKES,
   TO TASTE

¼ TEASPOON BLACK PEPPER

¼ TEASPOON SALT

TWO 6½-OUNCE CANS CHOPPED
   CLAMS, DRAINED

⅓ CUP CHOPPED PARSLEY

⅓ CUP GRATED PARMESAN CHEESE

1. In a large skillet, warm the oil with the butter over medium heat until the butter is melted. Add the onion and garlic, and cook, stirring frequently, until the onion is slightly brown, about 5 minutes.

2. Meanwhile, in a large pot of boiling water, cook the pasta until al dente according to package directions.

3. Add the flour to the onion mixture and cook, stirring constantly, until the flour is no longer visible, about 1 minute. Add the broth, red pepper flakes, black pepper, and salt. Reduce the heat to medium-low, cover, and simmer for 5 minutes.

4. Drain the pasta. Add the clams and parsley to the skillet and mix well. Add the pasta and toss to combine. Serve hot with the Parmesan on the side.

Variation: *For an interesting variation on this, use equal amounts of chopped basil and chopped cilantro in place of the parsley. This will give the dish a distinctly Thai flavor.*

Spaghettini with Spinach and Red Clam Sauce

SERVES 4

◆ EXTRA-QUICK

2 TABLESPOONS OLIVE OIL

2 TABLESPOONS UNSALTED BUTTER

1 MEDIUM ONION, COARSELY CHOPPED

3 GARLIC CLOVES, MINCED

2 TABLESPOONS FLOUR

1 POUND PLUM TOMATOES, COARSELY
  CHOPPED

ONE 8-OUNCE BOTTLE CLAM JUICE OR
  1 CUP CHICKEN BROTH

½ TEASPOON SALT

¼ TEASPOON BLACK PEPPER

½ POUND SPAGHETTINI OR SPAGHETTI

ONE 6½-OUNCE CAN CHOPPED CLAMS,
  DRAINED

4 CUPS (PACKED) FRESH SPINACH
  LEAVES, CHOPPED, OR ONE
  10-OUNCE PACKAGE FROZEN
  CHOPPED SPINACH, THAWED
  AND SQUEEZED DRY

⅔ CUP GRATED PARMESAN CHEESE

1. In a large skillet, warm the oil with the butter over medium-high heat until the butter is melted. Add the onion and garlic, and cook, stirring frequently, until the onion just begins to brown, 2 to 3 minutes. Stir in the flour and cook, stirring constantly, until the flour is no longer visible, about 30 seconds.

2. Stir in the tomatoes, clam juice, salt, and pepper. Bring the mixture to a boil. Reduce the heat to medium-low, cover, and simmer for 10 minutes.

3. Meanwhile, in a large pot of boiling water, cook the pasta until al dente according to package directions.

4. Increase the heat under the skillet to medium-high and bring the tomato mixture to a boil. Stir in the clams and spinach, and cook, stirring frequently, until the fresh spinach just wilts (or the frozen spinach is heated through), about 1 minute. Remove the pan from the heat.

5. Drain the pasta and transfer it to a large serving bowl. Add the spinach-clam sauce and ⅓ cup of the Parmesan and toss well to coat. Pass the remaining Parmesan on the side.

Fettuccine with Scallops and Cherry Tomatoes

SERVES 4

◇ LOW-FAT

1 TABLESPOON OLIVE OIL

1 MEDIUM ONION, COARSELY CHOPPED

3 GARLIC CLOVES, MINCED

¼ POUND MEDIUM MUSHROOMS, QUARTERED

1 PINT CHERRY TOMATOES

1 CUP NO-SALT-ADDED TOMATO SAUCE

1 TABLESPOON TOMATO PASTE

1 TEASPOON BASIL

½ TEASPOON THYME

¼ TEASPOON SALT

¼ TEASPOON BLACK PEPPER

¾ POUND FETTUCCINE OR OTHER BROAD NOODLES

1 SMALL YELLOW SQUASH, HALVED LENGTHWISE AND CUT CROSSWISE INTO THIN HALF-ROUNDS

½ POUND BAY SCALLOPS OR QUARTERED SEA SCALLOPS

⅓ CUP REDUCED-FAT SOUR CREAM

1. In a large skillet, warm the oil over medium-high heat. Add the onion and garlic, and cook, stirring frequently, until the mixture begins to brown, about 5 minutes.

2. Add the mushrooms, cherry tomatoes, tomato sauce, tomato paste, basil, thyme, salt, and pepper, and bring the mixture to a boil. Reduce the heat to low, cover, and simmer while you cook the pasta.

3. In a large pot of boiling water, cook the pasta until al dente according to package directions.

4. Increase the heat under the skillet to medium-high and return the tomato sauce to a boil. Add the squash and scallops, and cook, stirring constantly, until the scallops are just cooked through, about 4 minutes. Remove the pan from the heat. Stir in the sour cream until combined.

5. Drain the pasta well and divide it among 4 shallow bowls. Spoon the scallop mixture on top and serve hot.

PASTA SHELLS WITH GOLDEN BROILED SCALLOPS

SERVES 4

◆ EXTRA-QUICK   ◇ LOW-FAT

½ POUND MEDIUM PASTA SHELLS

1 TABLESPOON VEGETABLE OIL

1 CUP FINELY CHOPPED ONION

2 TABLESPOONS FLOUR

1½ CUPS CHICKEN BROTH, PREFERABLY
   REDUCED-SODIUM

¼ CUP HALF-AND-HALF

¼ TEASPOON SALT

¼ TEASPOON WHITE PEPPER

⅛ TEASPOON NUTMEG

¾ POUND SEA SCALLOPS

½ CUP GRATED PARMESAN CHEESE

3 TABLESPOONS UNSEASONED DRY
   BREAD CRUMBS

¼ TEASPOON PAPRIKA

1. In a large pot of boiling water, cook the pasta until al dente according to package directions.

2. Meanwhile, in a flameproof casserole or Dutch oven, warm the oil over medium heat. Add the onion and cook, stirring frequently, until softened, about 3 minutes. Stir in the flour and cook, stirring constantly, for 2 minutes.

3. Remove the casserole from the heat and gradually whisk in the broth and half-and-half, stirring until the sauce is smooth. Stir in the salt, pepper, and nutmeg, and set aside. Preheat the broiler.

4. Drain the pasta and add it to the sauce. Gently stir in the scallops. Return the casserole to the stove and bring the sauce to a simmer over medium heat. Reduce the heat to low, cover, and simmer until the scallops turn opaque, 2 to 3 minutes.

5. Sprinkle the scallop mixture with the Parmesan, bread crumbs, and paprika, and broil as close to the heat as possible for 2 minutes, or until the topping is golden. (If your broiler is beneath the oven, you may have to transfer the scallop mixture to a shallow baking dish or gratin dish for the broiling step.)

Angel Hair with Scallops and Basil Cream Sauce

SERVES 4

2 TABLESPOONS UNSALTED BUTTER

2 TABLESPOONS OLIVE OIL

1 TABLESPOON MINCED GARLIC

½ POUND SEA SCALLOPS, HALVED
   HORIZONTALLY

2 TABLESPOONS FRESH LEMON JUICE

½ POUND ANGEL HAIR PASTA

½ CUP HALF-AND-HALF

2 TABLESPOONS MINCED FRESH BASIL

2 TABLESPOONS MINCED CHIVES OR
   SCALLION GREENS

2 TABLESPOONS MINCED FRESH
   OREGANO, OR 2 TEASPOONS DRIED

½ TEASPOON SALT

¼ TEASPOON BLACK PEPPER

1 SMALL RED BELL PEPPER, CUT INTO
   THIN STRIPS

1 SMALL ZUCCHINI, CUT INTO THIN
   STRIPS

½ CUP GRATED PARMESAN CHEESE

1. In a large skillet, warm the oil with the butter over medium-high heat until the butter is melted. Add the garlic and scallops, and stir-fry until the scallops are opaque, about 3 minutes.

2. With a slotted spoon, transfer the scallop mixture to a medium bowl. Sprinkle with the lemon juice and cover with foil to keep warm. Reserve the oil and butter in the skillet.

3. In a large pot of boiling water, cook the pasta until al dente according to package directions.

4. Meanwhile, return the skillet to medium heat. When hot, add the half-and-half, basil, chives, oregano, salt, and black pepper. Bring to a boil and simmer gently until the sauce thickens, about 3 minutes.

5. Stir in the bell pepper and zucchini, and return the sauce to a boil. Remove from the heat.

6. Drain the pasta and return it to the pasta cooking pot. Add the basil cream sauce and the scallop mixture, and toss gently to combine. Divide the mixture among 4 serving plates and pass the Parmesan on the side.

Penne with Mixed Seafood

SERVES 4

♦ EXTRA-QUICK

3 TABLESPOONS OLIVE OIL

1 TABLESPOON UNSALTED BUTTER

1 MEDIUM ONION, COARSELY CHOPPED

1 POUND PENNE OR OTHER MEDIUM, TUBULAR PASTA

ONE 14½-OUNCE CAN NO-SALT-ADDED WHOLE TOMATOES

1 TABLESPOON CHOPPED FRESH BASIL, OR 1 TEASPOON DRIED

½ POUND LUMP CRABMEAT, PICKED OVER TO REMOVE ANY CARTILAGE

½ POUND BAY SCALLOPS OR QUARTERED SEA SCALLOPS

¼ POUND COOKED BABY SHRIMP

¼ TEASPOON SALT

¼ TEASPOON BLACK PEPPER

½ CUP GRATED PARMESAN CHEESE

1. In a large skillet, warm the oil with the butter over medium heat until the butter is melted. Add the onion and cook, stirring occasionally, until pale golden, 2 to 3 minutes.

2. In a large pot of boiling water, cook the pasta until al dente according to package directions.

3. Meanwhile, add the tomatoes and basil to the skillet, breaking up the tomatoes with the back of a spoon. Reduce the heat to low and simmer the mixture, stirring occasionally, for 10 minutes.

4. Add the crabmeat, scallops, and shrimp, and simmer until the scallops are cooked through, 2 to 3 minutes. Remove from the heat and season with the salt and pepper.

5. Drain the pasta and transfer it to a large serving bowl. Pour the seafood sauce on top and toss quickly to mix. Sprinkle with ¼ cup of the Parmesan and serve the remaining Parmesan on the side.

Penne with Crabmeat and Fresh Tomatoes

SERVES 4

2 TABLESPOONS OLIVE OIL

1 TABLESPOON UNSALTED BUTTER

2 MEDIUM ONIONS, CUT INTO THIN
WEDGES

3 GARLIC CLOVES, MINCED

6 MEDIUM PLUM TOMATOES, COARSELY
CHOPPED

¾ CUP SLICED BLACK OLIVES

¼ CUP (PACKED) CHOPPED FRESH DILL,
OR 1¼ TEASPOONS DRIED

¼ CUP (PACKED) CILANTRO SPRIGS,
MINCED

2 TABLESPOONS TOMATO PASTE

½ TEASPOON SALT

½ TEASPOON BLACK PEPPER

¼ TEASPOON SUGAR

¾ POUND PENNE OR OTHER MEDIUM,
TUBULAR PASTA

½ POUND LUMP CRABMEAT, PICKED
OVER TO REMOVE ANY CARTILAGE

1. In a medium skillet, warm the oil with the butter over medium-high heat until the butter is melted. Add the onions and garlic, and cook, stirring frequently, until the onions begin to brown, about 5 minutes.

2. Add the tomatoes, olives, dill, cilantro, tomato paste, salt, pepper, and sugar. Reduce the heat to low, cover, and simmer while you cook the pasta.

3. In a large pot of boiling water, cook the pasta until al dente according to package directions.

4. Drain the pasta and transfer it to a large serving bowl. Stir the crabmeat into the tomato mixture and spoon the mixture over the pasta. Toss well to combine and serve hot.

SWEET AFTERTHOUGHT: *Thread large strawberries and chunks of banana on skewers. Brush the fruit with orange liqueur (or honey mixed with a little orange juice) and broil until the strawberries are warm (do not overcook or they will fall off the skewers).*

FETTUCCINE WITH
SOLE AND YELLOW SQUASH

SERVES 4

◆ EXTRA - QUICK

½ POUND FETTUCCINE

1 TABLESPOON OLIVE OIL

1 TABLESPOON UNSALTED BUTTER

4 SCALLIONS, COARSELY CHOPPED

2 GARLIC CLOVES, MINCED

2 LARGE YELLOW SQUASH, HALVED
   LENGTHWISE AND CUT CROSSWISE
   INTO THIN HALF-ROUNDS

¼ CUP CHOPPED FRESH DILL, OR
   1 TABLESPOON DRIED

1 POUND SOLE FILLETS—OR ANY OTHER
   WHITE FISH SUCH AS RED SNAPPER—
   CUT INTO 1-INCH PIECES

½ CUP HALF-AND-HALF

½ TEASPOON SALT

¼ TEASPOON BLACK PEPPER

1. In a large pot of boiling water, cook the pasta until al dente according to package directions.

2. Meanwhile, in a large skillet, warm the oil with the butter over medium-high heat until the butter is melted. Add the scallions and garlic, and cook, stirring frequently, until the scallions are wilted, about 3 minutes.

3. Add the squash and dill, and cook, stirring frequently, until the squash begins to wilt, about 3 minutes.

4. Add the sole, half-and-half, salt, and pepper, and bring the mixture to a boil, stirring gently so as not to break up the fish. Cook until the sole just flakes when tested with a fork, about 3 minutes. Remove from the heat.

5. Drain the pasta and divide it among 4 shallow bowls. Spoon the sauce on top and serve hot.

FETTUCCINE WITH SWORDFISH AND ROASTED RED PEPPER

SERVES 4

¾ POUND SWORDFISH STEAK, CUT INTO
   ½-INCH CUBES
2 TABLESPOONS OLIVE OIL
1 TABLESPOON FRESH LEMON JUICE
2 GARLIC CLOVES, MINCED

1 MEDIUM RED BELL PEPPER, CUT INTO
   3 OR 4 FLAT PANELS, CORE AND
   SEEDS DISCARDED
¾ POUND FETTUCCINE
1 TABLESPOON CHOPPED PARSLEY

1. In a shallow glass baking dish, combine the swordfish, 1 tablespoon of the oil, the lemon juice, and garlic. Toss well, cover, and marinate at room temperature for 30 minutes.

2. Meanwhile, preheat the broiler. Place the pepper pieces, skin-side up, on a baking sheet and broil as close to the heat as possible for 10 minutes, or until evenly charred. Transfer the pepper pieces to a bowl and cover with a plate to steam the peppers. Preheat the oven to 400°.

3. When the peppers are cool enough to handle, peel them and slice into thin strips. Save any juices that have collected in the bowl.

4. Uncover the swordfish and bake for 6 to 8 minutes, or until just opaque.

5. Meanwhile, in a large pot of boiling water, cook the pasta until al dente according to package directions.

6. Drain the pasta and transfer it to a large serving bowl. Add the remaining 1 tablespoon oil, the roasted pepper and any juices, the parsley, and the swordfish and its cooking liquid. Toss gently to combine and serve hot.

Pasta Shells with Salmon in Lemon-Dill Cream

SERVES 4

♦ EXTRA-QUICK

½ POUND SMALL PASTA SHELLS

6 OUNCES NEUFCHÂTEL CREAM CHEESE

1 CUP PLAIN LOW-FAT YOGURT

1 TABLESPOON FRESH LEMON JUICE

1 TABLESPOON GRATED LEMON ZEST

¼ TEASPOON BLACK PEPPER

⅓ CUP CHOPPED FRESH DILL, OR
   2 TEASPOONS DRIED

ONE 10-OUNCE PACKAGE FROZEN PEAS

TWO 7½-OUNCE CANS SALMON,
   DRAINED AND FLAKED

1. In a large pot of boiling water, cook the pasta until al dente according to package directions.

2. Meanwhile, in a food processor, combine the cream cheese, yogurt, lemon juice, lemon zest, and pepper, and process until smooth. Transfer the mixture to a small bowl and stir in the dill. Set aside.

3. Place the frozen peas in a colander and pour the cooked pasta and boiling water over the peas.

4. Transfer the pasta and peas to a large serving bowl. Add the salmon and lemon-dill cream and toss gently to combine.

Kitchen Note: *To bring cold cream cheese quickly to room temperature (which makes it easier to blend), place the unwrapped cream cheese on a microwave-safe plate. Microwave at Medium until softened, about 1 minute (do this in 30-second increments).*

PEPPERS STUFFED WITH PASTA AND SALMON

SERVES 4

4 MEDIUM RED BELL PEPPERS
4 MEDIUM GREEN BELL PEPPERS
2 TABLESPOONS UNSALTED BUTTER
2 GARLIC CLOVES, MINCED
1 TEASPOON OREGANO
¼ TEASPOON BLACK PEPPER
4 CUPS COOKED MEDIUM PASTA SHAPES
   (ABOUT ½ POUND UNCOOKED)

¼ CUP GRATED PARMESAN CHEESE
¼ CUP SHREDDED PART-SKIM
   MOZZARELLA CHEESE
¼ CUP SLICED BLACK OLIVES
½ CUP REDUCED-FAT SOUR CREAM
ONE 7½-OUNCE CAN SALMON,
   DRAINED AND FLAKED

1. Preheat the oven to 375°. Butter a shallow baking dish large enough to hold the bell peppers snugly.

2. Slice off the bell pepper tops and discard. Scoop out the seeds and ribs. If necessary, slice a small piece off the bottoms of the peppers so they will stand upright. Place the peppers in the prepared baking dish.

3. In a small skillet, melt the butter over medium-high heat. Add the garlic and cook, stirring frequently, until fragrant, 2 to 3 minutes. Remove the skillet from the heat and stir in the oregano and black pepper.

4. In a medium bowl, combine the pasta, Parmesan, 2 tablespoons of the mozzarella, and the olives. Stir in the sour cream and garlic-oregano butter. Add the salmon and stir gently to combine.

5. Fill the peppers with the salmon-pasta mixture, dividing evenly. Sprinkle the tops with the remaining 2 tablespoons mozzarella. Bake for 25 to 30 minutes, or until the peppers are heated through and the cheese is melted.

BAKED PASTA WITH SALMON AND CHEDDAR SAUCE

SERVES 4

¾ POUND RADIATORE PASTA

4 TABLESPOONS UNSALTED BUTTER

2 GARLIC CLOVES, MINCED

⅓ CUP FLOUR

1¼ CUPS LOW-FAT MILK

1 CUP SHREDDED WHITE CHEDDAR
   CHEESE

1½ TEASPOONS DILL

½ TEASPOON SALT

¼ TEASPOON WHITE PEPPER

1 MEDIUM RED BELL PEPPER, DICED

1 MEDIUM GREEN BELL PEPPER, DICED

ONE 7½-OUNCE CAN SALMON,
   DRAINED AND FLAKED

3 TABLESPOONS GRATED PARMESAN
   CHEESE

1. Preheat the oven to 425°. Lightly grease a 13 x 9-inch baking dish.

2. In a large pot of boiling water, cook the pasta until al dente according to package directions.

3. Meanwhile, in a medium saucepan, melt the butter over medium heat. Add the garlic and cook, stirring frequently, until fragrant, about 1 minute. Add the flour and cook, stirring constantly, until the flour is no longer visible, about 30 seconds.

4. Gradually add the milk, stirring constantly to keep the sauce smooth. Stir in the Cheddar, dill, salt, and white pepper, and cook, stirring constantly, until the cheese is melted. Cover, remove from the heat, and set aside.

5. Drain the pasta and return it to the pasta cooking pot. Add the bell peppers, the cheese sauce, and the salmon, and stir gently to combine.

6. Spoon the mixture into the prepared baking dish. Sprinkle the top with the Parmesan. Bake for 15 minutes, or until heated through and beginning to brown on top.

FETTUCCINE WITH
SMOKED SALMON AND DILL SAUCE

SERVES 4

◆ EXTRA-QUICK

4 TABLESPOONS UNSALTED BUTTER
1 MEDIUM ONION, COARSELY CHOPPED
2 GARLIC CLOVES, MINCED
¾ POUND FETTUCCINE
¼ CUP FLOUR
1 CUP HALF-AND-HALF
½ CUP LOW-FAT MILK
⅓ CUP DRY WHITE WINE OR CHICKEN
    BROTH

⅓ CUP CHOPPED FRESH DILL, OR
    2½ TEASPOONS DRIED
½ TEASPOON SALT
¼ TEASPOON WHITE PEPPER
PINCH OF NUTMEG
¼ POUND SMOKED SALMON, CUT INTO
    BITE-SIZE PIECES
⅓ CUP GRATED PARMESAN CHEESE

1. In a medium saucepan, warm 2 tablespoons of the butter over medium-high heat until it is melted. Add the onion and garlic, and cook, stirring frequently, until the onion is softened but not browned, about 3 minutes.

2. In a large pot of boiling water, cook the pasta until al dente according to package directions.

3. Meanwhile, reduce the heat under the saucepan to medium. Add the remaining 2 tablespoons butter and warm until melted. Stir in the flour and cook, stirring constantly, until the flour is no longer visible, about 1 minute.

4. Stir in the half-and-half, milk, wine, dill, salt, pepper, and nutmeg, and bring the mixture to a simmer, stirring until smooth. Cook, stirring frequently, until the sauce is thickened, about 4 minutes. Remove from the heat and stir in the salmon and Parmesan.

5. Drain the pasta and transfer it to a large serving bowl. Spoon the salmon sauce on top and toss to combine. Serve hot.

Angel Hair Pasta with Veal, Mushrooms, and Peas

SERVES 4

♦ EXTRA-QUICK ◇ LOW-FAT

3 TABLESPOONS FLOUR

1 TEASPOON OREGANO

¼ TEASPOON SALT

¼ TEASPOON BLACK PEPPER

¾ POUND VEAL CUTLETS, CUT ACROSS
THE GRAIN INTO THIN STRIPS

½ POUND ANGEL HAIR PASTA OR
SPAGHETTINI

2 TABLESPOONS VEGETABLE OIL

2 TABLESPOONS UNSALTED BUTTER

1 MEDIUM ONION, COARSELY CHOPPED

2 GARLIC CLOVES, MINCED

½ POUND MUSHROOMS, HALVED

1 CUP CHICKEN BROTH

1 CUP FROZEN PEAS

¼ CUP GRATED PARMESAN CHEESE

1. In a plastic or paper bag, combine the flour, ½ teaspoon of the oregano, the salt, and pepper, and shake to mix. Add the veal and shake to coat. Remove the veal to a plate. Reserve 1 tablespoon of the seasoned flour.

2. In a large pot of boiling water, cook the pasta until al dente according to package directions.

3. Meanwhile, in a large skillet, warm 1 tablespoon of the oil with 1 tablespoon of the butter over medium-high heat until the butter is melted. Add the veal and stir-fry until browned, about 3 minutes. Transfer the veal to a plate and cover loosely to keep warm.

4. Add the remaining 1 tablespoon oil and 1 tablespoon butter to the skillet and warm over medium-high heat. Add the onion and garlic, and cook, stirring frequently, until the onion begins to brown, about 5 minutes.

5. Add the mushrooms and cook, stirring frequently, for 1 minute. Add the reserved seasoned flour and stir until the flour is no longer visible.

6. Add the broth, the remaining ½ teaspoon oregano, and the peas, and bring to a boil. Return the veal (and any juices that have collected on the plate) to the skillet and cook, stirring constantly, for 1 minute. Remove from the heat.

7. Drain the pasta and divide it among 4 serving plates. Spoon the veal mixture on top and pass the Parmesan on the side.

Meat Ravioli in Hearty Mushroom Broth

SERVES 4 TO 6

◆ EXTRA - QUICK

2 TABLESPOONS OLIVE OIL

1 MEDIUM ONION, THINLY SLICED

2 GARLIC CLOVES, MINCED

½ POUND MEDIUM MUSHROOMS, QUARTERED

2 TABLESPOONS FLOUR

1¾ CUPS BEEF BROTH

⅓ CUP DRY RED WINE OR BEEF BROTH

3 TABLESPOONS CHOPPED PARSLEY

1 TEASPOON BASIL

¼ TEASPOON BLACK PEPPER

1 POUND MEAT-FILLED RAVIOLI

1. In a large saucepan, warm the oil over medium-high heat. Add the onion and garlic, and cook, stirring frequently, until the onion begins to brown, about 3 minutes.

2. Add the mushrooms and cook, stirring frequently, for 1 minute. Stir in the flour and cook, stirring constantly, until the flour is no longer visible, about 30 seconds.

3. Stir in the broth, wine, parsley, basil, and pepper, and bring the mixture to a boil. Add the ravioli and cook until al dente according to package directions.

4. Divide the ravioli and broth among 4 shallow bowls and serve at once.

Variation: *If you can't find meat ravioli—or simply prefer a variation—you could prepare this dish with cheese ravioli, but substitute white wine for the red and chicken broth for the beef broth.*

PASTA WITH STIR-FRIED SESAME BEEF

SERVES 4 TO 6

3 TABLESPOONS ORIENTAL (DARK) SESAME OIL

2 TABLESPOONS REDUCED-SODIUM SOY SAUCE

¼ TEASPOON BLACK PEPPER

1¼ POUNDS FLANK STEAK, HALVED LENGTHWISE, THEN CUT ACROSS THE GRAIN INTO ¼-INCH-THICK SLICES

4 SCALLIONS, CUT INTO 2-INCH PIECES

3 GARLIC CLOVES, MINCED

3 MEDIUM CARROTS, THINLY SLICED

2 MEDIUM CELERY RIBS, THINLY SLICED

¼ CUP CHICKEN BROTH BLENDED WITH 2 TEASPOONS CORNSTARCH

4 DROPS HOT PEPPER SAUCE

3 TABLESPOONS CREAMY PEANUT BUTTER

2 TEASPOONS GRATED LEMON ZEST

1 TEASPOON FRESH LEMON JUICE

½ TEASPOON SUGAR

¼ TEASPOON RED PEPPER FLAKES

¾ POUND SPAGHETTINI OR CAPELLINI

¼ CUP CHOPPED CILANTRO

1. In a medium bowl, blend 1 tablespoon of the sesame oil, 1 tablespoon of the soy sauce, and the pepper. Add the beef slices and toss to coat. Cover and let marinate for 10 minutes.

2. In a large nonstick skillet, warm 1 tablespoon of the sesame oil over medium-high heat. Add the scallions and garlic, and stir-fry for 30 seconds. Add the beef and stir-fry until brown, about 4 minutes. Transfer the mixture to a plate and cover to keep warm.

3. Add the remaining 1 tablespoon sesame oil to the skillet and warm over medium-high heat. Stir in the carrots, celery, the cornstarch mixture, remaining 1 tablespoon soy sauce, hot pepper sauce, peanut butter, lemon zest, lemon juice, sugar, and red pepper flakes. Bring to a boil, stirring constantly. Reduce the heat to low, cover, and simmer for 5 minutes.

4. Meanwhile, in a large pot of boiling water, cook the pasta until al dente according to package directions.

5. Return the beef mixture to the skillet. Add the cilantro and cook, stirring, until the beef is hot, about 3 minutes. Remove from the heat.

6. Drain the pasta and divide it among 4 serving plates. Spoon the beef and sauce on top and serve hot.

Spaghetti with Broiled Steak Strips and Salsa

SERVES 4

2 MEDIUM FRESH TOMATOES, FINELY
   CHOPPED, OR ONE 14½-OUNCE CAN
   NO-SALT-ADDED WHOLE TOMATOES,
   DRAINED AND FINELY CHOPPED
4 SCALLIONS, FINELY CHOPPED
2 GARLIC CLOVES, MINCED
¼ CUP OLIVE OIL

2 TABLESPOONS RED WINE VINEGAR
1 TABLESPOON DIJON MUSTARD
¼ TEASPOON BLACK PEPPER
1 SMALL STRIP STEAK (¾ INCH THICK,
   ABOUT ¾ POUND)
½ POUND SPAGHETTI OR LINGUINE

1. Preheat the broiler.

2. In a medium bowl, combine the tomatoes, scallions, garlic, oil, vinegar, mustard, and pepper. Set aside half of the tomato salsa to toss with the cooked pasta.

3. Place the steak on a broiler pan. Divide the remaining tomato salsa in half again and spread it on the steak. Reserve the rest of the salsa baste. Broil the steak 4 inches from the heat for 7 minutes.

4. Meanwhile, in a large pot of boiling water, cook the pasta until al dente according to package directions.

5. Turn the steak over and spread with the reserved salsa baste. Broil for 7 minutes for rare; 9 minutes for medium-rare; and 11 minutes for medium to well-done. Transfer the steak to a cutting board and let it stand for 5 minutes.

6. Drain the pasta and transfer it to a large bowl. Add the reserved tomato salsa, toss to combine, and divide the mixture among 4 serving plates.

7. Cut the steak on the diagonal into thin slices. Place several steak slices on top of each portion of pasta and serve at once.

Egg Noodles with Beef, Scallions, and Snow Peas

SERVES 4

2 TABLESPOONS FRESH LIME JUICE

2 TEASPOONS HONEY

1½ TEASPOONS CURRY POWDER

½ POUND FINE EGG NOODLES

2 TABLESPOONS OLIVE OIL

½ POUND BONELESS BEEF SIRLOIN
   STEAK, CUT INTO STRIPS ABOUT
   1 INCH LONG AND ¼ INCH WIDE

1 GARLIC CLOVE, FINELY CHOPPED

¼ TEASPOON SALT

4 SCALLIONS, THINLY SLICED, WHITE
   AND GREEN PARTS KEPT SEPARATE

½ CUP CHICKEN BROTH

1 LARGE CARROT, HALVED LENGTHWISE
   AND CUT ON THE DIAGONAL INTO
   VERY THIN HALF-ROUNDS

¼ POUND SNOW PEAS, CUT ON THE
   DIAGONAL INTO THIRDS

1. In a small bowl, combine the lime juice, honey, and curry powder; set aside.

2. In a large pot of boiling water, cook the noodles until al dente according to package directions. Drain the noodles, transfer them to a large bowl, and toss with 1 tablespoon of the oil.

3. In a large skillet, warm the remaining 1 tablespoon oil over medium-high heat. Add the beef and stir-fry until seared, about 1 minute. Stir in the garlic, ⅛ teaspoon of the salt, the scallion whites, and the lime juice mixture, and stir-fry for 30 seconds. Add the beef mixture to the noodles and toss well to combine. Do not wash the skillet.

4. Return the skillet to medium-high heat and pour in the broth. Add the carrot and the remaining ⅛ teaspoon salt, and cook, scraping up any browned bits from the bottom of the skillet, for 3 minutes. Add the snow peas and cook, stirring, for 1 minute.

5. Add the vegetable mixture to the beef and noodles. Stir in the scallion greens and toss thoroughly to combine.

Moroccan Pasta
with Lamb and Sweet Spices

SERVES 4

2 TABLESPOONS VEGETABLE OIL

3 GARLIC CLOVES, MINCED

1 MEDIUM ONION, COARSELY CHOPPED

½ MEDIUM EGGPLANT, PEELED AND
   CUT INTO ½-INCH DICE

½ POUND LEAN GROUND LAMB

1½ TEASPOONS CINNAMON

1 TEASPOON CUMIN

½ TEASPOON SALT

½ TEASPOON GROUND GINGER

¼ TEASPOON RED PEPPER FLAKES

¼ TEASPOON BLACK PEPPER

PINCH OF CAYENNE PEPPER

2 MEDIUM PLUM TOMATOES, COARSELY
   CHOPPED

1 SMALL ZUCCHINI, THINLY SLICED

¾ POUND ORZO OR OTHER VERY SMALL
   PASTA SHAPE (ABOUT 2 CUPS)

½ CUP PITTED BLACK OLIVES, SLIVERED

½ CUP GOLDEN RAISINS

¼ CUP CHOPPED PARSLEY (OPTIONAL)

1. In a large nonstick skillet, warm the oil over medium-high heat. Add the garlic, onion, and eggplant, and cook, stirring frequently, until the onion begins to brown, about 5 minutes. Transfer the eggplant mixture to a plate and cover to keep warm.

2. Add the lamb to the skillet and cook, stirring frequently and breaking it up with a spoon, until the lamb is no longer pink, about 3 minutes.

3. Add the cinnamon, cumin, salt, ginger, red pepper flakes, black pepper, and cayenne. Cook, stirring constantly, until the spices are fragrant, about 1 minute.

4. Add the tomatoes and zucchini, and cook until the zucchini is slightly softened, 2 to 3 minutes. Return the eggplant mixture to the skillet, reduce the heat to low, cover, and simmer while you cook the pasta.

5. In a large pot of boiling water, cook the pasta until al dente according to package directions.

6. Stir the olives, raisins, and parsley (if using) into the lamb-eggplant sauce. Drain the pasta and divide it among 4 serving plates. Spoon the sauce on top and serve hot.

NOODLES WITH LAMB AND CARROTS

SERVES 4

◇ LOW-FAT

2 TABLESPOONS CORNSTARCH

¾ POUND LEAN BONELESS LAMB, CUT
INTO STRIPS 2 INCHES LONG AND
¼ INCH WIDE

2 TABLESPOONS OLIVE OIL

4 SCALLIONS, CUT INTO 1½-INCH
LENGTHS

3 GARLIC CLOVES, MINCED

3 MEDIUM CARROTS, THINLY SLICED

¾ CUP BEEF BROTH

2 TABLESPOONS CHOPPED FRESH MINT,
OR 2 TEASPOONS DRIED

2 TABLESPOONS FRESH LIME JUICE

1 TEASPOON GRATED LIME ZEST

1 TEASPOON HONEY

¼ TEASPOON BLACK PEPPER

¾ POUND THIN EGG NOODLES

1 CUP FROZEN PEAS

1. Place the cornstarch in a plastic bag. Add the lamb, shake to dredge the lamb lightly, and set aside.

2. In a large skillet, warm 1 tablespoon of the oil over medium-high heat. Add the scallions and garlic, and stir-fry until the garlic begins to color, about 3 minutes.

3. Add the remaining 1 tablespoon oil and the lamb, and stir-fry until the lamb is evenly browned, about 6 minutes. Transfer the lamb mixture to a plate and cover loosely to keep warm.

4. Add the carrots, broth, mint, lime juice, lime zest, honey, and pepper to the skillet. Stir well and bring the mixture to a boil. Reduce the heat to low, cover, and simmer while you cook the noodles.

5. In a large pot of boiling water, cook the noodles until al dente according to package directions.

6. About 3 minutes before the noodles are done, increase the heat under the skillet to medium-high and return the sauce to a boil. Return the lamb mixture (and any juices that have collected on the plate) to the skillet. Stir in the peas and cook until the peas are heated through, about 3 minutes. Remove from the heat.

7. Drain the noodles and divide them among 4 serving plates. Top with the lamb and vegetable mixture and serve at once.

Noodles with Pork Balls and Tomato-Pepper Sauce

SERVES 4

1 MEDIUM ONION, COARSELY CHOPPED

ONE 14½-OUNCE CAN NO-SALT-ADDED
  STEWED TOMATOES

3 GARLIC CLOVES, MINCED

1½ TEASPOONS OREGANO

1½ TEASPOONS BASIL

¼ TEASPOON BLACK PEPPER

¼ TEASPOON RED PEPPER FLAKES

1 BAY LEAF

¾ POUND GROUND PORK

½ CUP GRATED PARMESAN CHEESE

PINCH OF CAYENNE PEPPER

1 LARGE GREEN OR YELLOW BELL
  PEPPER, DICED

½ POUND WIDE EGG NOODLES

1. In a medium saucepan, combine the onion, stewed tomatoes, two-thirds of the garlic, ¾ teaspoon of the oregano, ¾ teaspoon of the basil, the black pepper, red pepper flakes, and bay leaf. Bring the mixture to a boil over medium-high heat. Reduce the heat to low, cover, and simmer while you prepare the meatballs.

2. In a bowl, combine the pork, ¼ cup of the Parmesan, the cayenne, and the remaining garlic, ¾ teaspoon oregano, and ¾ teaspoon basil. Using about 1 tablespoon of mixture for each, form the pork mixture into small balls.

3. Increase the heat under the saucepan to medium-high and bring the tomato sauce to a

boil. Add the pork balls and the bell pepper, and return the sauce to a boil. Reduce the heat to medium-low, cover, and simmer, stirring occasionally, for 15 minutes.

4. Meanwhile, in a large pot of boiling water, cook the noodles until al dente according to package directions.

5. Drain the noodles and divide them among 4 shallow bowls. Remove and discard the bay leaf from the tomato-pepper sauce. Spoon some of the sauce and pork balls on top of each portion of noodles. Serve with the remaining ¼ cup Parmesan on the side.

Szechuan Noodles with Pork and Vegetables

SERVES 4

¼ CUP (PACKED) CILANTRO SPRIGS

⅔ CUP BEEF BROTH

⅓ CUP CREAMY PEANUT BUTTER

3 TABLESPOONS ORIENTAL (DARK) SESAME OIL

3 TABLESPOONS WHITE VINEGAR

3 TABLESPOONS REDUCED-SODIUM SOY SAUCE

5 DROPS HOT PEPPER SAUCE

1 TABLESPOON LIGHT BROWN SUGAR

½ POUND LINGUINE OR SPAGHETTI

6 QUARTER-SIZE SLICES FRESH GINGER, MINCED

4 GARLIC CLOVES, MINCED

4 SCALLIONS, COARSELY CHOPPED

ONE 10-OUNCE PACKAGE FROZEN CUT GREEN BEANS, THAWED

2 MEDIUM CARROTS, CUT INTO 2-INCH MATCHSTICKS

¾ POUND WELL-TRIMMED PORK TENDERLOIN, CUT CROSSWISE INTO ¼-INCH-THICK SLICES

1. In a food processor, pulse the cilantro until coarsely chopped. Add the broth, peanut butter, 1 tablespoon of the sesame oil, the vinegar, soy sauce, hot pepper sauce, and brown sugar, and process until smooth. Set the peanut sauce aside.

2. In a large pot of boiling water, cook the pasta until al dente according to package directions.

3. Meanwhile, in a large skillet, warm 1 tablespoon of the sesame oil over medium-high heat. Add the ginger, garlic, and scallions, and stir-fry until the mixture begins to brown, about 3 minutes.

4. Add the remaining 1 tablespoon sesame oil and then add the green beans, carrots, and pork. Stir-fry until the pork is cooked through and the vegetables are crisp-tender, about 5 minutes.

5. Reduce the heat under the skillet to medium. Stir in the peanut sauce and bring the mixture to a boil. Remove from the heat.

6. Drain the pasta and transfer it to a large serving bowl. Add the pork mixture, toss well to combine, and serve hot.

Pork and Pepper Lo Mein

SERVES 4

◆ EXTRA-QUICK

3 TABLESPOONS CORNSTARCH

¾ POUND PORK TENDERLOIN, HALVED
LENGTHWISE THEN CUT CROSSWISE
INTO ¼-INCH-WIDE SLICES

1 CUP BEEF BROTH

2 TABLESPOONS REDUCED-SODIUM SOY
SAUCE

¼ TEASPOON BLACK PEPPER

½ POUND LINGUINE OR SPAGHETTI

¼ CUP VEGETABLE OIL

2 TEASPOONS ORIENTAL (DARK)
SESAME OIL

8 SCALLIONS, COARSELY CHOPPED

3 QUARTER-SIZE SLICES FRESH GINGER,
MINCED

2 GARLIC CLOVES, MINCED

¼ POUND MUSHROOMS, THINLY SLICED

1 LARGE RED BELL PEPPER, CUT INTO
THIN STRIPS

1. Spread the cornstarch in a shallow bowl. Dredge the pork in the cornstarch, reserving the excess cornstarch. Set the pork aside.

2. In a small bowl, combine the reserved cornstarch, broth, soy sauce, and black pepper, and stir to blend. Set the mixture aside.

3. In a large pot of boiling water, cook the pasta until al dente according to package directions.

4. Meanwhile, in a large skillet, warm 2 tablespoons of the vegetable oil and 1 teaspoon of the sesame oil over medium-high heat. Add the scallions, ginger, and garlic, and stir-fry until the scallions soften, 2 to 3 minutes.

5. Add the pork and stir-fry until the pork begins to brown, about 5 minutes. Transfer

the pork-scallion mixture to a plate and set aside.

6. Add the remaining 2 tablespoons vegetable oil and 1 teaspoon sesame oil to the skillet. Add the mushrooms and bell pepper, and stir-fry until the vegetables begin to wilt, about 5 minutes.

7. Stir the broth-cornstarch mixture to blend, then add to the skillet along with the pork-scallion mixture. Bring the mixture to a boil and cook, stirring constantly, until the sauce thickens slightly, about 2 minutes. Remove from the heat.

8. Drain the pasta and transfer it to a large serving bowl. Add the pork and vegetable mixture, toss to combine, and serve hot.

Spicy Noodles with Pork and Peanuts

SERVES 4

½ POUND LINGUINE, OR ¾ POUND
  FRESH ASIAN EGG NOODLES
1 TABLESPOON VEGETABLE OIL
2 SCALLIONS, FINELY CHOPPED
1 GARLIC CLOVE, MINCED
2 TEASPOONS MINCED FRESH GINGER
¼ TO ½ TEASPOON RED PEPPER FLAKES,
  TO TASTE
6 OUNCES WELL-TRIMMED PORK
  TENDERLOIN, FINELY CHOPPED
¼ CUP CHICKEN BROTH
¼ CUP DICED WATER CHESTNUTS

2 TABLESPOONS DRY SHERRY
1 TABLESPOON REDUCED-SODIUM SOY
  SAUCE
1 TEASPOON HOISIN SAUCE
¼ CUP UNSALTED DRY-ROASTED
  PEANUTS, COARSELY CHOPPED
¼ TEASPOON ORIENTAL (DARK) SESAME
  OIL
1 TABLESPOON CHOPPED CILANTRO
1 MEDIUM CUCUMBER—HALVED
  LENGTHWISE, SEEDED, AND CUT
  INTO MATCHSTICKS

1. In a large pot of boiling water, cook the pasta until al dente according to package directions. Drain, rinse under cold running water, and drain well. Set aside.

2. In a large skillet or wok, warm the vegetable oil over high heat. Add the scallions, garlic, ginger, and red pepper flakes, and stir-fry for 30 seconds. Add the pork and stir-fry until browned, about 3 minutes.

3. Add the broth, water chestnuts, sherry, soy sauce, and hoisin sauce, and stir-fry for 2 minutes. Stir in the peanuts and sesame oil. Add the pasta and toss until heated through, about 1 minute.

4. Transfer the pasta mixture to a large serving bowl. Sprinkle with the cilantro and garnish with the cucumber.

KITCHEN NOTE: *The pork tenderloin for this dish can be easily chopped in a food processor. However, if you are doing this by hand you may want to place the meat in the freezer for about 30 minutes in order to firm it up and make it easier to chop.*

Spaghettini with Sausage and Zucchini

SERVES 4

2 TABLESPOONS OLIVE OIL

½ SMALL ONION, FINELY CHOPPED

1 GARLIC CLOVE, MINCED

2½ CUPS CANNED NO-SALT-ADDED
WHOLE TOMATOES

½ TEASPOON SALT

¼ TEASPOON BLACK PEPPER

¼ TEASPOON BASIL

PINCH OF OREGANO

3 MEDIUM ZUCCHINI, THINLY SLICED

¾ POUND SWEET ITALIAN SAUSAGE,
CASINGS REMOVED

4 LARGE MUSHROOMS, THINLY SLICED

PINCH OF NUTMEG

3 TABLESPOONS DRY RED WINE OR
CHICKEN BROTH

1 POUND SPAGHETTINI

⅓ CUP GRATED PARMESAN CHEESE

1. In a medium saucepan, warm 1 tablespoon of the oil over medium heat. Add the onion and garlic, and cook, stirring frequently, until the onion is softened, about 5 minutes.

2. Add the tomatoes and break them up with the back of a spoon. Add ¼ teaspoon of the salt, the pepper, basil, and oregano. Bring the mixture to a boil, reduce the heat to low, and simmer, stirring frequently, for 20 minutes.

3. Meanwhile, in a large nonstick skillet, warm the remaining 1 tablespoon oil over medium heat. Add the zucchini and cook, stirring frequently, until golden brown. Transfer to a plate and set aside.

4. In the skillet over low heat, crumble in the sausage and cook, stirring frequently, until the sausage renders most of its fat. Pour off all but a thin layer of fat. Increase the heat to medium and cook, stirring frequently, until the sausage is browned. Add the mushrooms, remaining ¼ teaspoon salt, and the nutmeg. Add the wine and cook until it evaporates.

5. Add the zucchini and the sausage mixture to the tomato sauce and blend well. Let the sauce simmer while you cook the pasta.

6. In a large pot of boiling water, cook the pasta until al dente according to package directions.

7. Drain the pasta and transfer it to a large serving bowl. Add the sausage sauce and toss to combine. Pass the Parmesan on the side.

FETTUCCINE WITH CREAMY SAUSAGE SAUCE

SERVES 4

½ POUND HOT ITALIAN SAUSAGE,
   CASINGS REMOVED
2 MEDIUM ONIONS, MINCED
¼ POUND MUSHROOMS, THINLY SLICED
1 POUND FETTUCCINE OR PAPPARDELLE

2 TABLESPOONS UNSALTED BUTTER
¾ CUP HALF-AND-HALF
¼ TEASPOON SALT
¼ TEASPOON BLACK PEPPER
½ CUP GRATED PARMESAN CHEESE

1. In a medium nonstick skillet over low heat, crumble in the sausage and cook, stirring frequently, until the sausage renders its fat. Increase the heat to medium and add the onions. Cook, stirring frequently and breaking up the sausage, until the onions and sausage are browned, about 5 minutes.

2. Increase the heat to medium-high and add the mushrooms. Cook, stirring, until the mushrooms give up their liquid and the sausage is cooked through, about 5 minutes.

3. Meanwhile, in a large pot of boiling water, cook the pasta until al dente according to package directions.

4. In a small saucepan, melt the butter in ¼ cup of the half-and-half over medium heat. Bring the mixture just to a simmer, remove from the heat, and set aside.

5. Reduce the heat under the sausage mixture to medium. Stir in the salt, pepper, and the remaining ½ cup half-and-half. Bring to a boil, reduce the heat to low, and simmer until the sauce is slightly thickened, about 5 minutes. Remove from the heat.

6. Drain the pasta and transfer it to a large serving bowl. Add the warm half-and-half mixture and toss to combine. Add the sausage sauce and the Parmesan and toss again.

Ziti with Roasted Peppers and Hot Sausage

SERVES 4

◇ LOW-FAT

3 MEDIUM RED BELL PEPPERS, CUT
   INTO 3 OR 4 FLAT PANELS, CORE
   AND SEEDS DISCARDED
¼ POUND HOT ITALIAN SAUSAGE,
   CASINGS REMOVED
2 GARLIC CLOVES, MINCED
2 TEASPOONS FRESH THYME, OR
   ½ TEASPOON DRIED

½ POUND ZITI OR OTHER SHORT,
   TUBULAR PASTA
1½ CUPS CANNED CRUSHED TOMATOES
1 TABLESPOON RED WINE VINEGAR
⅛ TEASPOON SALT

1. Preheat the broiler. Place the pepper pieces, skin-side up, on a baking sheet and broil as close to the heat as possible for 10 minutes, or until evenly charred. Transfer the pepper pieces to a bowl and cover with a plate to steam the peppers. Set aside.

2. In a medium nonstick skillet, crumble in the sausage over medium-high heat. Cook, stirring frequently and breaking up the sausage, until the sausage is browned, about 3 minutes. Remove the pan from the heat and stir in the garlic and thyme.

3. In a large pot of boiling water, cook the pasta until al dente according to package directions.

4. Meanwhile, peel the peppers and slice them lengthwise into thin strips. Return the sausage mixture to medium heat and stir in the pepper strips, tomatoes, vinegar, and salt. Bring to a simmer and cook the sauce until slightly thickened, 5 to 7 minutes. Remove from the heat.

5. Drain the pasta and return it to the cooking pot. Add the sausage-roasted pepper sauce and toss well to combine. Cover the pot and let the mixture stand for 5 minutes to allow the flavors to blend.

Spaghetti Timbale

SERVES 4

¾ POUND SWEET ITALIAN SAUSAGE,
CASINGS REMOVED

3 GARLIC CLOVES, MINCED

1 MEDIUM ONION, COARSELY CHOPPED

¾ POUND SPAGHETTI

1 CUP LOW-FAT COTTAGE CHEESE

½ CUP REDUCED-FAT SOUR CREAM

2 EGGS

1½ TEASPOONS OREGANO

¾ TEASPOON NUTMEG

½ TEASPOON SALT

½ TEASPOON BLACK PEPPER

1 CUP SHREDDED MONTEREY JACK
CHEESE

¼ CUP CHOPPED PARSLEY (OPTIONAL)

1. Preheat the oven to 375°. Lightly grease and flour an 8½-inch springform pan.

2. In a medium skillet over medium heat, cook the sausage with the garlic and onion, stirring frequently to crumble, until the sausage is no longer pink, about 7 minutes. Remove the skillet from the heat and drain off the sausage fat.

3. In a large pot of boiling water, cook the pasta until al dente according to package directions.

4. Meanwhile, in a large mixing bowl with an electric mixer, beat the cottage cheese until smooth. Beat in the sour cream, eggs, oregano, nutmeg, salt, and pepper until combined.

5. Drain the spaghetti well and add it to the cottage cheese mixture. Add the sausage-

onion mixture, ½ cup of the Monterey jack cheese, and the parsley (if using). Toss to combine well.

6. Spoon the mixture into the prepared springform pan and sprinkle with the remaining ½ cup Monterey jack cheese. Cover with foil and bake for 20 minutes, or until heated through.

7. Preheat the broiler. Remove the foil from the timbale. Broil the timbale 4 inches from the heat for 5 to 7 minutes, or until golden on top.

8. Let the timbale stand for about 5 minutes before unmolding. To unmold, run a knife around the edges of the timbale and then release the sides of the springform. Cut the timbale into wedges to serve.

Macaroni with Pepper-Pepperoni Sauce

SERVES 4

ONE 16-OUNCE CAN CRUSHED
   TOMATOES
ONE 8-OUNCE CAN TOMATO SAUCE
3 GARLIC CLOVES, MINCED
1½ TEASPOONS OREGANO
¼ TEASPOON BLACK PEPPER
6 OUNCES PEPPERONI, CASINGS
   REMOVED AND CUT INTO
   ⅓-INCH CUBES
1 LARGE CARROT, COARSELY CHOPPED

1 LARGE RED BELL PEPPER, DICED
1 MEDIUM RED ONION, COARSELY
   CHOPPED
¼ CUP (PACKED) FRESH BASIL LEAVES,
   FINELY CHOPPED, OR 1½
   TEASPOONS DRIED BASIL
¾ POUND SMALL ELBOW MACARONI
1 CUP SHREDDED PART-SKIM
   MOZZARELLA CHEESE

1. In a medium saucepan, combine the crushed tomatoes, tomato sauce, garlic, oregano, and black pepper. Bring the mixture to a boil over medium-high heat. Reduce the heat to low, cover, and simmer for 5 minutes.

2. Stir in the pepperoni, carrot, bell pepper, onion, and basil, and return the mixture to a boil over medium-high heat. Reduce the heat to low, cover, and simmer while you cook the pasta.

3. In a large pot of boiling water, cook the pasta until al dente according to package directions.

4. Drain the pasta and transfer it to a large serving bowl. Add the pepper-pepperoni sauce and toss well to combine. Serve at once, passing the mozzarella separately.

Variation: *Try another hard sausage in place of the pepperoni, such as Italian soppressata or Latin American chorizo (make sure you get the cured not the fresh version of chorizo).*

Linguine with Smoked Ham and Herb Butter

SERVES 4

♦ EXTRA-QUICK

¾ POUND LINGUINE OR SPAGHETTI

4 TABLESPOONS UNSALTED BUTTER

2 MEDIUM ONIONS, COARSELY
CHOPPED

3 GARLIC CLOVES, MINCED

1 TABLESPOON OLIVE OIL

3 MEDIUM CARROTS, THINLY SLICED

1 MEDIUM YELLOW SQUASH, THINLY
SLICED

¼ CUP CHOPPED PARSLEY (OPTIONAL)

2 TABLESPOONS SHREDDED FRESH
BASIL, OR 2 TEASPOONS DRIED

2 TEASPOONS OREGANO

½ POUND SMOKED HAM, CUT INTO
½-INCH CUBES

1 CUP FROZEN PEAS, THAWED

¼ TEASPOON BLACK PEPPER

1. In a large pot of boiling water, cook the pasta until al dente according to package directions.

2. Meanwhile, in a large skillet, melt 2 tablespoons of the butter over medium-high heat. Add the onions and garlic, and cook, stirring frequently, until the onions begin to brown, about 3 minutes.

3. Add the remaining 2 tablespoons butter, the oil, carrots, squash, parsley (if using),

basil, and oregano. Cook, stirring constantly, until the vegetables are almost tender, about 4 minutes.

4. Add the ham and peas, and cook, stirring frequently, until the ham and peas are heated through and the vegetables are tender. Stir in the pepper. Remove from the heat.

5. Drain the pasta and transfer it to a large serving bowl. Add the ham and vegetable sauce, toss well to combine, and serve at once.

Kitchen Note: *Heating herbs in butter brings out their full flavor; the butter then carries the herb flavor throughout the dish. If your family does not use butter, do not substitute margarine. Use a good quality olive oil instead and add about ¼ teaspoon of salt.*

Pasta Shells
with Spinach and Ham

SERVES 4

2 TEASPOONS UNSALTED BUTTER

1 SMALL ONION, FINELY CHOPPED

2 GARLIC CLOVES, MINCED

2 CUPS CHICKEN BROTH, PREFERABLY
REDUCED-SODIUM

¼ CUP DRY VERMOUTH OR DRY WHITE
WINE

¼ CUP HALF-AND-HALF

1 BAY LEAF

¼ TEASPOON BLACK PEPPER

PINCH OF NUTMEG

½ POUND MEDIUM PASTA SHELLS

1 POUND FRESH SPINACH, STEMMED
AND COARSELY TORN

2 OUNCES BAKED OR BOILED HAM,
JULIENNED

1. In a large skillet, melt the butter over medium-high heat. Add the onion and garlic, and cook, stirring frequently, until the onion is softened, about 5 minutes.

2. Add the broth, vermouth, half-and-half, bay leaf, pepper, and nutmeg, and cook until approximately 1 cup of the liquid remains, 10 to 15 minutes. Remove and discard the bay leaf.

3. Meanwhile, in a large pot of boiling water, cook the pasta until al dente according to package directions.

4. About 3 minutes before the pasta is done, stir the spinach and ham into the broth mixture, cover, and cook for 3 minutes. Uncover and stir the mixture until the spinach is completely wilted, about 30 seconds. Remove from the heat.

5. Drain the pasta and immediately add it to the skillet. Stir well to combine and let the mixture stand for 1 minute to blend the flavors. Stir well again just before serving.

Noodles with Asparagus and Canadian Bacon

SERVES 4

3 TABLESPOONS OLIVE OIL

1 MEDIUM ONION, FINELY CHOPPED

¼ POUND BUTTON MUSHROOMS,
THINLY SLICED, OR 2 OUNCES FRESH
SHIITAKE MUSHROOMS, STEMMED
AND THINLY SLICED

2 GARLIC CLOVES, MINCED

¼ TEASPOON BLACK PEPPER

½ POUND WIDE EGG NOODLES

½ POUND THIN ASPARAGUS, CUT ON
THE DIAGONAL INTO 3-INCH PIECES

15 FRESH BASIL LEAVES, CUT INTO
THIN STRIPS

1½ OUNCES CANADIAN BACON, CUT
INTO THIN STRIPS

1 TEASPOON FRESH LEMON JUICE

½ CUP GRATED PARMESAN CHEESE

1. In a large skillet, warm 1 tablespoon of the oil over medium-high heat. Add the onion and cook, stirring frequently, until softened, about 5 minutes.

2. Add the button mushrooms, garlic, and pepper, and cook, stirring frequently, until the mushrooms give up their liquid, about 10 minutes.

3. Meanwhile, in a large pot of boiling water, cook the noodles until al dente according to package directions.

4. Add the asparagus to the mushroom mixture and cook until the asparagus is tender, 4 to 5 minutes. Stir in the basil, Canadian bacon, and lemon juice, and remove the pan from the heat.

5. Drain the noodles and immediately add them to the skillet. Add the Parmesan and the remaining 2 tablespoons oil, and toss well to combine. Serve hot.

PASTA WITH MUSHROOMS AND BACON

SERVES 4

6 SLICES BACON

1 MEDIUM ONION, COARSELY CHOPPED

3 GARLIC CLOVES, MINCED

½ POUND ZITI OR OTHER MEDIUM, TUBULAR PASTA

2 TEASPOONS FLOUR

½ POUND SMALL MUSHROOMS

ONE 16-OUNCE CAN CRUSHED TOMATOES

2 TABLESPOONS TOMATO PASTE

1½ TEASPOONS THYME

¼ TEASPOON BLACK PEPPER

½ CUP HALF-AND-HALF

1. In a large skillet, cook the bacon over medium heat until crisp, about 10 minutes. Drain the bacon on paper towels, crumble, and set aside. Pour off all but a thin film of bacon fat.

2. Add the onion and garlic to the skillet and cook, stirring frequently, until the onion begins to brown, about 5 minutes.

3. In a large pot of boiling water, cook the pasta until al dente according to package directions.

4. Meanwhile, add the flour to the skillet and cook, stirring constantly, until the flour is no longer visible, about 1 minute. Add the mushrooms, crushed tomatoes, tomato paste, thyme, and pepper, increase the heat to medium-high, and bring the mixture to a boil. Reduce the heat to low and simmer for 5 minutes.

5. Return the mushroom mixture to a boil over medium-high heat, add the half-and-half, and cook, stirring constantly, until the mixture is heated through, about 1 minute. Remove from the heat.

6. Drain the pasta and transfer it to a large serving bowl. Add the mushroom sauce and the crumbled bacon, toss well to combine, and serve at once.

Warm Macaroni Salad with Artichokes

SERVES 4

◆ EXTRA-QUICK

½ POUND ELBOW MACARONI

2 TABLESPOONS OLIVE OIL

1 MEDIUM ONION, COARSELY CHOPPED

3 GARLIC CLOVES, MINCED

½ POUND ASPARAGUS, CUT INTO
    2-INCH LENGTHS

2 LARGE CARROTS, THINLY SLICED

ONE 10-OUNCE PACKAGE FROZEN
    ARTICHOKE HEARTS, THAWED

1 CUP FROZEN PEAS

⅓ CUP REDUCED-FAT MAYONNAISE

¼ CUP GRATED PARMESAN CHEESE

2 TABLESPOONS DIJON MUSTARD

¼ TEASPOON BLACK PEPPER

1. In a large pot of boiling water, cook the pasta until al dente according to package directions.

2. Meanwhile, in a large skillet, warm 1 tablespoon of the oil over medium-high heat. Add the onion and garlic, and cook, stirring frequently, until the garlic begins to brown, about 3 minutes.

3. Add the remaining 1 tablespoon oil to the skillet. Stir in the asparagus, carrots, artichoke hearts, and peas, and cook, stirring occasionally, until the asparagus and carrots are tender, 7 to 9 minutes.

4. In a large serving bowl, stir together the mayonnaise, Parmesan, mustard, and pepper.

5. Drain the pasta well. Add the hot pasta and the vegetable mixture to the mustard sauce and toss well to coat.

SWEET AFTERTHOUGHT: *For dessert, serve a Peach Melba Sundae: Purée a package of thawed frozen raspberries in a food processor or blender (if desired, strain out the seeds). Stir in a scant tablespoon of a fruit-based liqueur, such as Grand Marnier. Spoon the raspberry sauce over peach ice cream.*

Rotini with Spring Vegetables

SERVES 4

◇ LOW-FAT

1 CUP CHICKEN BROTH, PREFERABLY
  REDUCED-SODIUM
½ POUND FRESH BUTTON MUSHROOMS
  OR SHIITAKE MUSHROOMS, DICED
1 LARGE ONION, CUT INTO 8 CHUNKS
½ TEASPOON SALT
2 TABLESPOONS OLIVE OIL
¼ CUP RED WINE VINEGAR

2 TABLESPOONS FRESH LEMON JUICE
3 MEDIUM CARROTS, CUT ON THE
  DIAGONAL INTO ½-INCH SLICES
½ POUND ASPARAGUS, CUT ON THE
  DIAGONAL INTO 1-INCH LENGTHS
½ POUND ROTINI
¼ CUP THINLY SLICED FRESH BASIL
¼ TEASPOON BLACK PEPPER

1. In a large skillet, combine ¾ cup of the broth, the mushrooms, onion, and ¼ teaspoon of the salt. Bring the mixture to a boil over medium heat, reduce the heat to low, cover, and cook for 5 minutes.

2. Uncover the mixture and cook, stirring frequently, until all the broth has evaporated. Stir in 1 tablespoon of the oil and cook for 3 minutes. Transfer to a large serving bowl.

3. Add the vinegar and the remaining ¼ cup broth to the skillet. Bring to a boil over medium-high heat, stirring to loosen any browned bits, and cook until the liquid is reduced to approximately 2 tablespoons. Add the liquid to the mushroom mixture.

4. In a large saucepan, combine 2 quarts of water and 1 tablespoon of the lemon juice, and bring to a boil over medium-high heat.

Add the carrots and cook until crisp-tender, about 6 minutes. Add the asparagus and cook for 30 seconds. Reserve the cooking water for the pasta and, with a slotted spoon, transfer the vegetables to a colander. Rinse the vegetables under cold running water, drain, and add them to the mushroom mixture.

5. Return the reserved cooking water to a boil. Add the pasta and the remaining 1 tablespoon lemon juice, and cook the pasta until al dente according to package directions. Drain the pasta, rinse under cold running water, and drain well.

6. Add the pasta to the vegetable mixture along with the remaining 1 tablespoon oil, the basil, the remaining ¼ teaspoon salt, and the pepper. Toss to combine and serve.

Tortellini Salad with Lemon-Mustard Vinaigrette

SERVES 4

◆ EXTRA - QUICK

6 OUNCES CHEESE-FILLED TORTELLINI

2 TABLESPOONS FRESH LEMON JUICE

1 TEASPOON GRATED LEMON ZEST

¼ CUP OLIVE OIL

1 TABLESPOON DIJON MUSTARD

½ TEASPOON DILL

⅛ TEASPOON SALT

⅛ TEASPOON BLACK PEPPER

PINCH OF SUGAR

6 CHERRY TOMATOES, HALVED

1 SMALL RED OR YELLOW BELL PEPPER, CUT INTO BITE-SIZE PIECES

1 SMALL GREEN BELL PEPPER, CUT INTO BITE-SIZE PIECES

1 SMALL ZUCCHINI, CUT INTO MATCHSTICKS

½ SMALL RED ONION, THINLY SLICED

3 SCALLIONS, FINELY CHOPPED

1. In a large pot of boiling water, cook the tortellini until al dente according to package directions.

2. Meanwhile, in a large serving bowl, combine the lemon juice and zest. Whisk in the oil, mustard, dill, salt, black pepper, and sugar.

3. Drain the tortellini, add them to the lemon-mustard vinaigrette, and toss to coat.

4. Add the cherry tomatoes, bell peppers, zucchini, red onion, and scallions, and toss well to combine. Serve the salad warm or at room temperature.

Kitchen Note: *This salad is ideally suited to being made ahead. Follow the recipe as directed, but in Step 2 remove about half of the vinaigrette and set aside. Toss the pasta and vegetables with the dressing remaining in the bowl and refrigerate until serving time. Before serving, toss the salad with the reserved vinaigrette.*

Warm Pasta Salad with Sautéed Vegetables

SERVES 4

◆ EXTRA-QUICK   ◇ LOW-FAT

½ POUND SMALL PASTA SHELLS OR
   ORZO
2 TABLESPOONS VEGETABLE OIL
1 MEDIUM RED ONION, COARSELY
   CHOPPED
3 CLOVES GARLIC, MINCED
1 LARGE CARROT, COARSELY CHOPPED
1 MEDIUM ZUCCHINI, COARSELY
   CHOPPED

3 TABLESPOONS FRESH LEMON JUICE
2 TABLESPOONS DIJON MUSTARD
1 TEASPOON OREGANO
½ TEASPOON SALT
½ TEASPOON BLACK PEPPER
½ POUND COOKED TURKEY OR HAM,
   CUT INTO ½-INCH DICE
⅓ CUP GRATED PARMESAN CHEESE

1. In a large pot of boiling water, cook the pasta until al dente according to package directions.

2. Meanwhile, in a large skillet, warm 1 tablespoon of the oil over medium-high heat. Add the onion and garlic, and cook, stirring frequently, until the onion begins to brown, about 5 minutes.

3. Add the remaining 1 tablespoon oil to the skillet. Add the carrot and zucchini, and cook, stirring frequently, until the carrot is just tender, about 5 minutes. Remove from the heat.

4. In a large serving bowl, whisk together the lemon juice, mustard, oregano, salt, and pepper.

5. Drain the pasta, add it to the dressing, and toss to coat. Add the sautéed vegetables, diced turkey, and Parmesan, and toss well to combine. Serve the pasta salad warm or at room temperature

Pasta Salad with Chicken, Eggplant, and Squash

SERVES 4

◇ LOW-FAT

2½ TABLESPOONS FRESH LIME JUICE

2 TABLESPOONS OLIVE OIL

1 MEDIUM EGGPLANT, HALVED LENGTHWISE AND CUT CROSSWISE INTO ½-INCH-THICK HALF-ROUNDS

½ POUND PASTA TWISTS

1 LARGE YELLOW SQUASH, CUT INTO ½-INCH-THICK HALF-ROUNDS

2 SHALLOTS OR 1 SMALL ONION, FINELY CHOPPED

½ POUND SKINLESS, BONELESS CHICKEN BREASTS, CUBED

¼ TEASPOON THYME

¼ TEASPOON SALT

2 LARGE PLUM TOMATOES, CUT INTO ¼-INCH-WIDE WEDGES

2 OUNCES SOFT GOAT CHEESE

¼ CUP PLAIN LOW-FAT YOGURT

2 TABLESPOONS MILK

¼ TEASPOON BLACK PEPPER

1. Preheat the broiler.

2. In a cup, mix 1 tablespoon of the lime juice with 1 tablespoon of the oil, and brush the mixture over both sides of the eggplant slices. Set the slices on a baking sheet and broil for 6 to 8 minutes, turning once, or until lightly browned. Let the slices cool slightly, then transfer to a large bowl and refrigerate.

3. In a large pot of boiling water, cook the pasta until al dente according to package directions. Drain, rinse under cold running water, and drain well. Add to the eggplant.

4. Meanwhile, in a large skillet, warm the remaining 1 tablespoon oil over medium-high heat. Add the squash and shallots, and stir-fry for 1 minute.

5. Add the remaining 1½ tablespoons lime juice, the chicken, thyme, and salt. Stir-fry until the chicken is cooked through, about 5 minutes. Add the tomatoes and stir-fry for 30 seconds. Add to the eggplant mixture.

6. In a food processor or blender, process the goat cheese, yogurt, milk, and pepper until puréed. Add the dressing to the pasta salad, toss to coat, and chill briefly before serving.

SHELLS WITH TOMATOES AND CHUNKS OF CHICKEN

SERVES 4

◇ LOW-FAT

½ POUND SKINLESS, BONELESS
CHICKEN BREASTS, CUT INTO
1-INCH CHUNKS
½ TEASPOON CINNAMON
¼ TEASPOON SALT
¼ TEASPOON BLACK PEPPER

2 LARGE SHALLOTS, THINLY SLICED
1½ POUNDS TOMATOES, SEEDED AND
COARSELY CHOPPED
1 TABLESPOON GRATED ORANGE ZEST
½ POUND MEDIUM SPINACH PASTA
SHELLS

1. Arrange the chicken in a single layer in a large pie plate or shallow heatproof bowl. Sprinkle with the cinnamon, salt, and pepper. Scatter the shallot slices evenly over the chicken and top with the tomatoes. Sprinkle the orange zest on top and cover the plate tightly with foil.

2. Pour enough water into a medium saucepan to make it one-third full. Bring the water to a rolling boil. Set the covered plate on top of the saucepan like a lid and cook the chicken until it is no longer pink and the

meat feels firm but springy to the touch, 5 to 8 minutes. Remove the plate from the saucepan and uncover it.

3. Meanwhile, in a large pot of boiling water, cook the pasta until al dente according to package directions.

4. Drain the pasta and transfer it to a large serving bowl. Add the chicken-tomato sauce and toss well to combine. Serve warm or at room temperature.

VARIATION: *To give this a Tex-Mex kick, replace the cinnamon with cumin; replace the shallots with 1 clove minced garlic and 3 chopped scallions; and add a pinch of cayenne.*

PASTA SALAD WiTH ASPARAGUS AND SHRiMP

SERVES 4

1 LARGE RED BELL PEPPER, CUT INTO
    3 OR 4 FLAT PANELS
24 THIN ASPARAGUS SPEARS, CUT ON
    THE DIAGONAL INTO ½-INCH PIECES
½ POUND MEDIUM SHRIMP, SHELLED
    AND DEVEINED
¾ POUND LINGUINE
2 GARLIC CLOVES, MINCED

2½ TABLESPOONS FRESH LEMON JUICE
2 TABLESPOONS CHOPPED PARSLEY
2 TEASPOONS DIJON MUSTARD
1 TEASPOON GRATED LEMON ZEST
¼ TEASPOON SALT
¼ TEASPOON BLACK PEPPER
⅓ CUP OLIVE OIL
1 CUP PITTED BLACK OLIVES, HALVED

1. Preheat the broiler. Place the bell pepper pieces, skin-side up, on a baking sheet and broil as close to the heat as possible for 10 minutes, or until evenly charred. Transfer the pepper pieces to a bowl; cover with a plate to steam them. When they are cool enough to handle, peel the pepper pieces, cut them into thin strips, and set aside.

2. Meanwhile, in a saucepan with a steamer insert, steam the asparagus over 1 inch of boiling water until crisp-tender, 5 to 6 minutes. Reserving the cooking liquid, remove the steamer insert and spread the asparagus on a towel to cool.

3. Return the cooking liquid to a boil. Remove from the heat and add the shrimp; stir, cover, and let stand until the shrimp are just curled, 3 to 5 minutes. Transfer the shrimp to

the towel to cool. Measure 3 tablespoons of the cooking liquid and discard the remainder. Split the shrimp lengthwise and set aside.

4. In a large pot of boiling water, cook the pasta until al dente according to package directions. Drain, rinse under cold running water, and drain well. Transfer the pasta to a large serving bowl.

5. In a medium bowl, whisk together the reserved 3 tablespoons cooking liquid, the garlic, lemon juice, parsley, mustard, lemon zest, salt, and black pepper. Gradually whisk in the oil.

6. Pour the dressing over the pasta. Add the bell pepper, asparagus, shrimp, and olives, and toss to combine.

PASTA SALAD
WITH AVOCADO DRESSING

SERVES 4

♦ EXTRA-QUICK

½ POUND SMALL PASTA SHELLS

1 MEDIUM AVOCADO, HALVED AND
PITTED

¾ CUP REDUCED-FAT MAYONNAISE

2 TABLESPOONS CIDER VINEGAR

1 TEASPOON DIJON MUSTARD

½ TEASPOON SALT

¼ TEASPOON BLACK PEPPER

¼ POUND BAKED HAM, CUT INTO
½-INCH CUBES

3 MEDIUM CELERY RIBS, CUT INTO
½-INCH DICE

2 MEDIUM TOMATOES, CUT INTO
½-INCH DICE

1. In a large pot of boiling water, cook the pasta until al dente according to package directions. Drain the pasta, rinse it under cold running water, and drain well. Transfer the pasta to a large serving bowl.

2. Meanwhile, scoop out the avocado meat and place it in a medium bowl. With a fork, mash the avocado until smooth. Stir in the mayonnaise, vinegar, mustard, salt, and pepper.

3. Add the ham, celery, and tomatoes to the pasta and toss gently to combine. Add the avocado dressing and toss gently to evenly coat the ingredients.

SUBSTITUTIONS: *The recipe for this simple pasta salad is extremely flexible. If you do not have ham, use 1 cup of cubed cooked turkey or chicken. If you do not have celery, use 1 cup of diced green, yellow, or red bell pepper. The rich and creamy avocado dressing is delicious, but if you are counting calories, you may want to substitute low-fat yogurt for some or all of the mayonnaise.*

CURRIED PASTA SALAD WITH TOMATOES AND SHRIMP

SERVES 4

◇ LOW-FAT

½ POUND BOW TIE PASTA OR OTHER
FANCY PASTA SHAPE

1 LARGE STALK BROCCOLI, CUT INTO
BITE-SIZE PIECES

2 MEDIUM CARROTS, CUT INTO BITE-
SIZE PIECES

½ POUND MEDIUM SHRIMP, SHELLED
AND DEVEINED

¼ CUP (PACKED) CILANTRO SPRIGS

1 CUP LOW-FAT COTTAGE CHEESE

1 CUP PLAIN LOW-FAT YOGURT

2 TABLESPOONS FRESH LIME JUICE

1 TO 2 TABLESPOONS CURRY POWDER

1 TEASPOON GRATED LIME ZEST

¼ TEASPOON SUGAR

¼ TEASPOON SALT

⅛ TEASPOON BLACK PEPPER

1 PINT CHERRY TOMATOES, HALVED

1. In a large pot of boiling water, cook the pasta until al dente according to package directions.

2. While the pasta is cooking, place a colander over the boiling water and add the broccoli and carrots; cover the colander and steam the vegetables until crisp-tender, 3 to 4 minutes. Remove the colander, rinse the vegetables under cold running water, and drain well.

3. About 5 minutes before the pasta is done, add the shrimp to the pasta cooking water and cook until just opaque.

4. Meanwhile, in a food processor, process the cilantro until minced. Add the cottage cheese and process until smooth. Add the yogurt, lime juice, curry powder, lime zest, sugar, salt, and pepper, and process until combined.

5. Drain the pasta and shrimp and transfer them to a large serving bowl. Add the cherry tomatoes, broccoli, carrots, and curry sauce, and toss gently to combine. Serve the salad warm, at room temperature, or chilled.

SWEET-AND-SOUR CURLY NOODLE AND HAM SALAD

SERVES 4

6 OUNCES CURLY EGG NOODLES

½ CUP REDUCED-FAT MAYONNAISE

¼ CUP VEGETABLE OIL

8 TO 10 SCALLIONS, THINLY SLICED, WHITE AND GREEN PARTS KEPT SEPARATE

1 SMALL GREEN OR RED BELL PEPPER, CUT INTO THIN STRIPS

¼ CUP CIDER VINEGAR

2 TABLESPOONS DARK BROWN SUGAR

½ TEASPOON SALT

¼ TEASPOON BLACK PEPPER

½ POUND SMOKED HAM, THINLY SLICED AND CUT INTO THIN RIBBONS

8 TO 10 RADISHES, THINLY SLICED

2 MEDIUM CELERY RIBS, SLICED ON THE DIAGONAL INTO THIN STRIPS

½ HEAD OF ICEBERG LETTUCE, THINLY SHREDDED

1 PINT CHERRY TOMATOES

1. In a large pot of boiling water, cook the noodles until al dente according to package directions. Drain the noodles and transfer them to a large heatproof bowl. Add the mayonnaise and toss to coat.

2. In a small skillet, warm the oil over medium heat. Add the scallion whites and the bell pepper strips, and cook, stirring constantly, until the pepper strips are slightly softened, about 2 minutes. Add the vinegar and brown sugar, and stir until the brown sugar dissolves and the liquid comes to a boil. Remove from the heat and add the salt and black pepper.

3. Using a spatula, fold the hot scallion mixture into the noodles, then fold in the ham, radishes, and celery.

4. Arrange the shredded lettuce on a serving platter. Heap the warm salad in the center of the lettuce, and garnish with the scallion greens and cherry tomatoes.

Vermicelli Salad with Sliced Pork

SERVES 4

◆ EXTRA-QUICK ◇ LOW-FAT

½ POUND VERMICELLI OR
   SPAGHETTINI, BROKEN INTO THIRDS
1½ TEASPOONS VEGETABLE OIL
¼ POUND WELL-TRIMMED PORK LOIN,
   POUNDED FLAT AND CUT INTO THIN
   STRIPS
2 GARLIC CLOVES, MINCED
4 MEDIUM RIBS CELERY, CUT INTO
   THIN MATCHSTICKS
3 MEDIUM CARROTS, CUT INTO THIN
   MATCHSTICKS

2 TABLESPOONS RICE WINE VINEGAR OR
   1½ TABLESPOONS CIDER VINEGAR
2 TEASPOONS ORIENTAL (DARK)
   SESAME OIL
1 TEASPOON CREAM SHERRY
   (OPTIONAL)
6 DROPS HOT PEPPER SAUCE
¼ TEASPOON SALT
¼ TEASPOON BLACK PEPPER

1. In a large pot of boiling water, cook the pasta until al dente according to package directions. Drain and rinse under cold running water.

2. Meanwhile, in a large nonstick skillet, warm the vegetable oil over medium-high heat. Add the pork and stir-fry for 2 minutes. Add the garlic and stir-fry until fragrant, about 30 seconds. Add the celery and carrots, and stir-fry until vegetables are crisp-tender and the pork is cooked through, about 2 minutes. Remove from the heat.

3. In a small bowl, combine the vinegar, sesame oil, sherry (if using), hot pepper sauce, salt, and black pepper.

4. Transfer the pasta to a large serving bowl. Add the pork-vegetable mixture and the dressing, and toss to combine. Serve the salad at room temperature or chilled.

SPAGHETTI WITH TWO CHEESES

SERVES 4

◆ EXTRA-QUICK

1 POUND SPAGHETTI

1 TABLESPOON OLIVE OIL

⅓ CUP GRATED PARMESAN OR ASIAGO CHEESE

⅓ CUP GRATED ROMANO CHEESE

¼ TEASPOON BLACK PEPPER

4 TABLESPOONS UNSALTED BUTTER, CUT INTO SMALL BITS

2 TABLESPOONS HALF-AND-HALF

1. In a large pot of boiling water, cook the pasta with the oil until the pasta is al dente according to package directions.

2. Meanwhile, in a small bowl, combine the Parmesan, Romano, and pepper, and stir with a fork to blend.

3. Ladle out about ½ cup of the pasta cooking water and set aside. Drain the pasta well in a colander.

4. Add the butter and half-and-half to the pasta cooking pot. Add the pasta and toss gently until evenly coated. Add half of the cheese mixture and toss to combine. If the mixture seems dry, add enough of the reserved pasta cooking water to moisten. Pass the remaining cheese mixture at the table.

SWEET AFTERTHOUGHT: *For a fast dessert, peel 4 apples and cut into large chunks. In a medium covered saucepan, bring the apples and about 2 tablespoons of liquid such as water or apple juice to a boil. Reduce the heat to a vigorous simmer and cook, stirring once or twice, until the apples are completely soft (this will only be 5 to 10 minutes). Mash the apples lightly and serve warm with ice cream or sweetened sour cream.*

FETTUCCINE WITH RICH BLUE CHEESE SAUCE

SERVES 4 TO 6

◆ EXTRA-QUICK

1 POUND SPINACH FETTUCCINE OR
   REGULAR FETTUCCINE
¼ POUND GORGONZOLA OR OTHER
   RICH BLUE CHEESE

3 TABLESPOONS UNSALTED BUTTER
¼ CUP MILK
¾ CUP HALF-AND-HALF
1 CUP GRATED PARMESAN CHEESE

1. In a large pot of boiling water, cook the pasta until almost al dente according to package directions.

2. About 3 minutes before the pasta is done, in a flameproof casserole, mash the Gorgonzola over low heat and stir in the butter until melted and well combined.

3. Stir in the milk and cook, stirring constantly, until the mixture is thick and creamy, about 1 minute. Stir in the half-and-half until thoroughly combined.

4. Drain the pasta well and add it to the Gorgonzola sauce. Add ½ cup of the Parmesan and toss to combine. Serve immediately with the remaining Parmesan on the side.

KITCHEN NOTES: *Because this recipe is made with two cheeses that can be fairly salty, it is important to use freshly grated Parmesan—either the refrigerated pre-grated type available in most supermarkets, or a chunk of cheese to be grated at home. Freshly grated Parmesan has a higher moisture content and a sweeter, nuttier taste. The unrefrigerated grated Parmesan in canisters tends to be too salty when used in large quantities, as here.*

Spaghettini with Mushroom-Herb Sauce

SERVES 4

2 TABLESPOONS OLIVE OIL

1 TABLESPOON UNSALTED BUTTER

¾ CUP CHOPPED SHALLOTS OR
    SCALLION WHITES

3 GARLIC CLOVES, MINCED

¾ POUND MUSHROOMS, THINLY SLICED

2 TABLESPOONS FLOUR

¾ CUP CHICKEN BROTH

1 TEASPOON BASIL

½ TEASPOON TARRAGON

¼ TEASPOON BLACK PEPPER

¾ POUND SPAGHETTINI OR SPAGHETTI

½ CUP HALF-AND-HALF

3 TABLESPOONS CHOPPED CHIVES OR
    SCALLION GREENS

½ CUP GRATED PARMESAN CHEESE

1. In a large skillet, warm 1 tablespoon of the oil with the butter over medium-high heat until the butter is melted. Add the shallots and garlic, and cook, stirring frequently, until the shallots start to brown, about 5 minutes.

2. Add the remaining 1 tablespoon oil and the mushrooms, and cook, stirring frequently, until the mushrooms begin to soften, 3 to 5 minutes.

3. Add the flour and stir until the flour is no longer visible, about 30 seconds. Add the broth, basil, tarragon, and pepper, and bring the mixture to a boil, stirring constantly. Reduce the heat to low, cover, and simmer for 10 minutes.

4. Meanwhile, in a large pot of boiling water, cook the pasta until al dente according to package directions.

5. Increase the heat under the skillet to medium-high and return the mushroom mixture to a boil. Add the half-and-half, reduce the heat to medium, and cook, uncovered, for 2 minutes. Remove from the heat and stir in the chives.

6. Drain the pasta and transfer it to a large serving bowl. Add the mushroom-herb sauce and a sprinkling of the Parmesan, and toss to combine. Pass the remaining Parmesan on the side.

PASTA WITH TRIPLE TOMATO SAUCE

SERVES 4

◆ EXTRA-QUICK

¾ POUND LINGUINE OR SPAGHETTI

3 TABLESPOONS OIL FROM THE SUN-
DRIED TOMATOES OR OLIVE OIL

4 SCALLIONS, COARSELY CHOPPED

2 GARLIC CLOVES, MINCED

⅓ CUP (PACKED) FRESH BASIL LEAVES,
CHOPPED, OR 1 TABLESPOON DRIED
BASIL

1 TEASPOON OREGANO

¼ TEASPOON RED PEPPER FLAKES

¼ TEASPOON BLACK PEPPER

ONE 8-OUNCE CAN NO-SALT-ADDED
TOMATO SAUCE

8 OIL-PACKED SUN-DRIED TOMATO
HALVES, COARSELY CHOPPED

6 CANNED NO-SALT-ADDED WHOLE
TOMATOES, COARSELY CHOPPED

1. In a large pot of boiling water, cook the pasta until al dente according to package directions.

2. Meanwhile, in a small skillet, warm the oil over medium-high heat. Add the scallions and garlic, and cook, stirring frequently, until the garlic is fragrant, about 2 minutes.

3. Stir in the basil, oregano, red pepper flakes, and black pepper, and remove the pan from the heat.

4. Drain the pasta and transfer it to a large serving bowl. Add the tomato sauce, sun-dried tomatoes, canned tomatoes, and scallion-herb oil, and toss gently to combine. Serve warm or at room temperature.

SUBSTITUTION: *If you would prefer to use non-oil-packed sun-dried tomatoes, chop them as directed above, but soften them first by letting them sit in boiling water for about 10 minutes. In place of the sun-dried tomato oil called for, use 3 tablespoons of olive oil and add about ¼ teaspoon salt in Step 3.*

Linguine with Meat Sauce

SERVES 4

1 TEASPOON OLIVE OIL

1 SMALL ONION, COARSELY CHOPPED

3 GARLIC CLOVES, MINCED

¾ POUND LEAN GROUND BEEF

ONE 14½-OUNCE CAN NO-SALT-ADDED
    WHOLE TOMATOES

ONE 8-OUNCE CAN TOMATO SAUCE

½ TEASPOON BASIL

½ TEASPOON OREGANO

½ TEASPOON ROSEMARY, CRUMBLED

½ TEASPOON THYME

¼ TEASPOON RED PEPPER FLAKES

¼ TEASPOON BLACK PEPPER

1 BAY LEAF

¾ POUND LINGUINE OR SPAGHETTI

½ CUP GRATED PARMESAN CHEESE

1. In a medium saucepan, warm the oil over medium-high heat. Add the onion and garlic, and cook, stirring frequently, until the onion begins to brown, 2 to 3 minutes.

2. Crumble in the ground beef and cook, stirring frequently, until the beef is no longer pink, about 4 minutes.

3. Add the tomatoes, breaking them up with a spoon. Stir in the tomato sauce, basil, oregano, rosemary, thyme, red pepper flakes, black pepper, and bay leaf. Bring the mixture to a boil over medium-high heat. Reduce the heat to low and simmer, stirring occasionally, for 15 minutes.

4. Meanwhile, in a large pot of boiling water, cook the pasta until al dente according to package directions.

5. Drain the pasta and transfer it to a large serving bowl. Remove and discard the bay leaf from the sauce, pour the sauce over the pasta, and toss to combine. Serve at once, passing the Parmesan on the side.

Bow Ties with Tomatoes and Ground Beef

SERVES 4

2 TEASPOONS OLIVE OIL

½ POUND LEAN GROUND BEEF

1 LARGE GREEN BELL PEPPER, FINELY
CHOPPED

1 MEDIUM ONION, FINELY CHOPPED

3 GARLIC CLOVES, MINCED

TWO 16-OUNCE CANS NO-SALT-ADDED
WHOLE TOMATOES IN TOMATO
PURÉE

2 TABLESPOONS TOMATO PASTE

1 BAY LEAF

1 TEASPOON BASIL

1 TEASPOON OREGANO

½ TEASPOON SALT

¼ TEASPOON BLACK PEPPER

½ POUND BOW TIE PASTA OR OTHER
FANCY PASTA SHAPE

½ CUP SHREDDED PART-SKIM
MOZZARELLA CHEESE

1. In a large nonstick skillet, warm the oil over medium heat. Crumble in the ground beef and cook, stirring frequently, until the meat is no longer pink, about 5 minutes.

2. Add the bell pepper, onion, and garlic, and cook, stirring frequently, until the onion is beginning to brown, about 8 minutes.

3. Add the tomatoes, breaking them up with the back of a spoon. Stir in the tomato paste, bay leaf, basil, oregano, salt, and black pepper. Increase the heat to medium-high and bring the mixture to a boil. Reduce the heat to medium-low, cover, and simmer until the sauce has thickened, 15 to 20 minutes.

4. Meanwhile, in a large pot of boiling water, cook the pasta until al dente according to package directions.

5. Drain the pasta and transfer it to a large serving bowl. Remove and discard the bay leaf from the sauce. Pour the sauce over the pasta and toss to combine. Divide the mixture among 4 shallow bowls, sprinkle with the mozzarella, and serve hot.

BAKED ZITI WITH HAM AND CHEESE

SERVES 4

½ POUND ZITI OR OTHER SHORT,
    TUBULAR PASTA
4 TABLESPOONS UNSALTED BUTTER
3 TABLESPOONS FLOUR
2½ CUPS LOW-FAT MILK
2 CUPS SHREDDED EXTRA-SHARP
    CHEDDAR CHEESE

½ TEASPOON SALT
½ TEASPOON BLACK PEPPER
½ POUND BAKED OR BOILED HAM, CUT
    INTO ¼-INCH CUBES
PINCH OF PAPRIKA

1. Preheat the oven to 375°. Lightly butter a shallow baking dish.

2. In a large pot of boiling water, cook the pasta until almost al dente according to package directions.

3. Meanwhile, in a medium saucepan, melt 3 tablespoons of the butter over medium heat. Stir in the flour and cook, stirring constantly, until the mixture is bubbly, about 3 minutes. Remove the pan from the heat and whisk in the milk to blend well.

4. Return the pan to the heat and cook, stirring, until the sauce is slightly thickened. Add 3 tablespoons of the Cheddar and stir until melted. Stir in the salt and pepper.

5. Drain the pasta well and return it to the pasta cooking pot. Add the cream sauce and the ham, and toss well to combine.

6. Spread a layer of the pasta mixture in the prepared baking dish. Sprinkle with a dusting of paprika and a layer of the Cheddar. Repeat layering, ending with the Cheddar. Dot with the remaining 1 tablespoon butter and bake for 25 to 30 minutes, or until bubbling.

Variation: *For the spicy food lovers in your family, try this simple baked pasta with pepper jack cheese instead of Cheddar. And, for an extra flavor twist, replace the ham with smoked turkey.*

STAR-STUFFED BELL PEPPERS

SERVES 4

6 OUNCES SKINLESS, BONELESS
   CHICKEN BREASTS, CUT INTO SMALL
   PIECES

3 SCALLIONS, THINLY SLICED

1½ TABLESPOONS COARSELY CHOPPED
   FRESH GINGER

1 GARLIC CLOVE, MINCED

2 TABLESPOONS VEGETABLE OIL

ONE 3-OUNCE JAR PIMIENTOS,
   DRAINED AND FINELY CHOPPED

2 TEASPOONS DISTILLED WHITE
   VINEGAR

½ TEASPOON SALT

¼ TEASPOON BLACK PEPPER

1¼ CUPS SMALL STAR-SHAPED PASTA

4 LARGE RED BELL PEPPERS

1 TEASPOON ORIENTAL (DARK) SESAME
   OIL

1. Preheat the oven to 350°. Butter a shallow baking dish large enough to hold the bell peppers snugly upright.

2. On a cutting board, mound together the chicken pieces, scallions, ginger, and garlic, and chop them into fine pieces.

3. In a large nonstick skillet, warm the vegetable oil over medium heat. Add the chicken mixture and cook, breaking it up with a wooden spoon, until the chicken turns white, about 4 minutes. Stir in the pimientos, vinegar, ¼ teaspoon of the salt, and the black pepper. Remove the pan from the heat.

4. In a large pot of boiling water, cook the pasta until al dente according to package directions. Drain the pasta and stir it into the chicken mixture.

5. Slice off the bell pepper tops and set the tops aside. Scoop out the seeds and ribs. If necessary, slice a small piece off the bottoms of the peppers so they will stand upright. Rub the insides of the peppers with the sesame oil, then sprinkle with the remaining ¼ teaspoon salt.

6. Fill the peppers with the chicken-pasta mixture and replace their tops. Reserve any stuffing that does not fit. Place the stuffed peppers in the prepared baking dish and bake for 25 minutes.

7. Remove the dish from the oven and distribute the reserved stuffing around the peppers. Bake for 5 to 10 minutes, or until the bell peppers and the extra stuffing are heated through.

Macaroni and Cheddar Bake

SERVES 4

½ POUND SMALL ELBOW MACARONI

1 CUP COTTAGE CHEESE

1 TABLESPOON Dijon MUSTARD

⅔ CUP SOUR CREAM

½ TEASPOON BLACK PEPPER

2 CUPS SHREDDED SHARP Cheddar
CHEESE

ONE 10-OUNCE PACKAGE FROZEN
PEAS, THAWED

3 TABLESPOONS MINCED CHIVES OR
SCALLION GREENS

1. Preheat the oven to 400°. Butter a shallow 1½-quart baking dish.

2. In a large pot of boiling water, cook the pasta until al dente according to package directions.

3. Meanwhile, in a food processor or blender, process the cottage cheese and mustard until smooth. Transfer the cottage cheese mixture to a large bowl and stir in the sour cream and pepper.

4. Drain the pasta well and add it to the cottage cheese mixture. Add 1½ cups of the Cheddar, the peas, and chives, and stir until well combined.

5. Spoon the mixture into the prepared baking dish and sprinkle it with the remaining ½ cup Cheddar. Bake for about 25 minutes, or until lightly browned on top.

KITCHEN NOTE: *In this variation on this classic American dish, green peas add color and texture, while cottage cheese and sour cream replace the usual white sauce. To cut calories, use low-fat cottage cheese and reduced-calorie sour cream. There really is no substitute, however, for tantalizingly sharp Cheddar cheese.*

Macaroni with Tuna and Mushroom Sauce

SERVES 4

♦ EXTRA-QUICK

½ POUND SMALL ELBOW MACARONI

1¼ CUPS CHICKEN BROTH, PREFERABLY
REDUCED-SODIUM

2 GARLIC CLOVES, MINCED

1 LARGE RED BELL PEPPER, CUT INTO
THIN STRIPS

½ POUND SMALL MUSHROOMS, HALVED

4 TABLESPOONS UNSALTED BUTTER

⅓ CUP FLOUR

¾ TEASPOON OREGANO

¼ TEASPOON BLACK PEPPER

1 CUP FROZEN PEAS

½ CUP REDUCED-FAT SOUR CREAM

ONE 6⅛-OUNCE CAN WATER-PACKED
TUNA, DRAINED AND COARSELY
FLAKED

1. In a large pot of boiling water, cook the pasta until al dente according to package directions.

2. Meanwhile, in a medium saucepan, bring the broth to a boil over medium-high heat. Add the garlic, bell pepper, and mushrooms, cover, and return to a boil. Reduce the heat to medium-low and simmer for 5 minutes.

3. Meanwhile, in another medium saucepan, melt the butter over medium heat. Stir in the flour and cook, stirring constantly, until the flour is no longer visible, about 1 minute.

4. Stir in the oregano and black pepper. Add the mushroom mixture and stir to blend well. Stir in the peas and cook until heated through, 2 to 3 minutes. Remove from the heat and stir in the sour cream.

5. Drain the pasta and add it to the sauce. Toss well to coat. Gently stir in the tuna, taking care to leave it somewhat chunky.

Substitution: *Almost any kind of fish would work well with this simple pasta dish. Use canned salmon in place of the tuna. Or, if you have leftover cooked fish—firm types such as halibut, cod, or swordfish are best—flake it into medium-size chunks and add it to the pasta at the end.*

SHRIMP SCAMPI OVER LINGUINE

SERVES 4

◇ LOW-FAT

¾ POUND LINGUINE OR SPAGHETTI

1 TABLESPOON CORNSTARCH

½ CUP PLUS 1 TABLESPOON CHICKEN
   BROTH

1 TABLESPOON OLIVE OIL

1 TABLESPOON UNSALTED BUTTER

5 SCALLIONS, COARSELY CHOPPED

4 GARLIC CLOVES, MINCED

1 POUND MEDIUM SHRIMP, SHELLED
   AND DEVEINED

2 MEDIUM TOMATOES, COARSELY
   CHOPPED

¼ CUP CHOPPED PARSLEY

½ TEASPOON SALT

¼ TEASPOON BLACK PEPPER

PINCH OF SUGAR

1. In a large pot of boiling water, cook the pasta until al dente according to package directions.

2. Meanwhile, in a cup, combine the cornstarch and 1 tablespoon of the broth. Stir to combine and set aside.

3. In a large skillet, warm the oil with the butter over medium-high heat until the butter is melted. Add the scallions and garlic, and cook, stirring frequently, until the scallions are wilted, about 1 minute. Add the shrimp and cook, stirring frequently, until they turn pink and are opaque, about 5 minutes.

4. Add the tomatoes, the remaining ½ cup broth, parsley, salt, pepper, and sugar, and bring to a boil, stirring constantly. Add the reserved cornstarch mixture and cook, stirring constantly, until the shrimp are cooked through and the sauce is thickened, 1 to 2 minutes. Remove from the heat.

5. Drain the pasta and transfer it to a large serving bowl. Spoon the shrimp mixture on top, toss to combine, and serve hot.

Spinach Pasta with Cauliflower-Cheddar Sauce

SERVES 4

◆ EXTRA-QUICK

¾ POUND SPINACH LINGUINE OR
    SPINACH FETTUCCINE
1 SMALL HEAD OF CAULIFLOWER, CUT
    INTO BITE-SIZE PIECES
4 TABLESPOONS UNSALTED BUTTER
2 GARLIC CLOVES, MINCED
⅓ CUP FLOUR

½ CUP CHICKEN BROTH
1 CUP LOW-FAT MILK
2 CUPS SHREDDED SHARP CHEDDAR
    CHEESE
3 TABLESPOONS DIJON MUSTARD
¼ TEASPOON BLACK PEPPER

1. In a large pot of boiling water, cook the pasta until al dente according to package directions. About 5 minutes before the pasta is done, add the cauliflower to the boiling water and cook until just tender.

2. Meanwhile, in a medium saucepan, melt the butter over medium heat. Add the garlic and cook, stirring frequently, for 1 minute. Add the flour and cook, stirring constantly, until the flour absorbs all the butter.

3. Gradually pour the broth into the saucepan and stir until the sauce is smooth. Stir in the milk until well combined. Add the Cheddar, mustard, and pepper, and stir until the cheese is melted. Remove the cheese sauce from the heat.

4. Drain the pasta and cauliflower and transfer them to a large serving bowl. Add the cheese sauce, toss well to coat, and serve.

Kitchen Note: *The flavorful sauce for this dish is made with sharp Cheddar cheese. Look for a well-aged Cheddar, which will have the deepest flavor; using your palate and pocketbook as your guides, choose one from New York State, Wisconsin, or Vermont, or select an imported English cheese. The color of the Cheddar makes no difference to its taste, although by tradition in this country white Cheddars tend to be on the sharper side.*

Vegetable Lo Mein

SERVES 4

◇ LOW-FAT

¾ POUND LINGUINE OR SPAGHETTI

⅔ CUP CHICKEN BROTH

¼ CUP REDUCED-SODIUM SOY SAUCE

1 TABLESPOON CORNSTARCH

1 TABLESPOON DRY SHERRY (OPTIONAL)

3 DROPS HOT PEPPER SAUCE

¼ TEASPOON RED PEPPER FLAKES

¼ TEASPOON BLACK PEPPER

2 TABLESPOONS VEGETABLE OIL

5 SLICES FRESH GINGER, MINCED

3 GARLIC CLOVES, MINCED

4 SCALLIONS, COARSELY CHOPPED

1 LARGE RED BELL PEPPER, CHOPPED

½ SMALL HEAD OF CABBAGE,
  SHREDDED

¼ POUND MUSHROOMS, QUARTERED

¼ POUND FRESH SPINACH, STEMMED
  AND ROUGHLY TORN

¼ POUND BEAN SPROUTS

¼ CUP CILANTRO SPRIGS, MINCED

1. In a large pot of boiling water, cook the pasta until al dente according to package directions.

2. Meanwhile, in a small bowl, combine the broth, soy sauce, cornstarch, sherry (if using), hot pepper sauce, red pepper flakes, and black pepper. Stir to blend and set aside.

3. In a large skillet or wok, warm 1 tablespoon of the oil over medium-high heat. Add the ginger and garlic, and stir-fry until fragrant, about 2 minutes.

4. Add the remaining 1 tablespoon oil and then the scallions, bell pepper, cabbage, mushrooms, spinach, and bean sprouts. Stir-fry until the vegetables begin to soften, about 4 minutes.

5. Drain the pasta and add it to the skillet. Stir in the cornstarch-broth mixture and the cilantro, and cook, stirring constantly, until the mixture is heated through and slightly thickened, about 2 minutes. Serve hot.

WAGON WHEEL PASTA SALAD

SERVES 4

◇ LOW-FAT

8 SUN-DRIED (NOT OIL-PACKED)
   TOMATO HALVES
½ CUP BOILING WATER
ONE 10-OUNCE PACKAGE FROZEN BABY
   LIMA BEANS
1 POUND WAGON WHEEL PASTA OR
   OTHER FANCY PASTA SHAPE

2 GARLIC CLOVES, PEELED
¼ CUP RED WINE VINEGAR
¼ TEASPOON SALT
¼ TEASPOON BLACK PEPPER
4 CHERRY TOMATOES, QUARTERED
2 TABLESPOONS MINCED CHIVES
1 TABLESPOON OLIVE OIL

1. In a small heatproof bowl, combine the sun-dried tomatoes and the boiling water and let the tomatoes stand until softened, about 15 minutes.

2. Meanwhile, in a medium saucepan of water, cook the lima beans until tender according to package directions. Drain the beans, rinse under cold running water, and drain well. Transfer the beans to a large serving bowl.

3. In a large pot of boiling water, cook the pasta until al dente according to package directions. Drain the pasta, rinse under cold running water, and drain well. Add the pasta to the lima beans.

4. In a blender or food processor, process the sun-dried tomatoes along with their soaking liquid, the garlic, vinegar, salt, and pepper until puréed.

5. Add the tomato-garlic purée to the pasta mixture and toss to coat. Add the cherry tomatoes, chives, and oil, and toss again.

Substitution: *For the lima bean haters in your family, make this salad instead with a 10-ounce package of frozen cut green beans or yellow wax beans. Once they are thawed, be sure to drain them well on paper towels or they will make the salad soggy.*

Pasta Primavera Salad

SERVES 4

◆ EXTRA-QUICK ◇ LOW-FAT

½ CUP (PACKED) FRESH BASIL LEAVES,
MINCED, OR 2 TEASPOONS DRIED
BASIL
3 TABLESPOONS OLIVE OIL
2 TABLESPOONS FRESH LEMON JUICE
1 TABLESPOON DIJON MUSTARD
2 TEASPOONS GRATED LEMON ZEST
½ TEASPOON SALT
¼ TEASPOON BLACK PEPPER
¼ TEASPOON RED PEPPER FLAKES

½ POUND EGG NOODLES
3 GARLIC CLOVES, PEELED
ONE 10-OUNCE PACKAGE FROZEN PEAS
ONE 10-OUNCE PACKAGE FROZEN
ASPARAGUS SPEARS
4 MEDIUM PLUM TOMATOES, COARSELY
CHOPPED
3 SCALLIONS, COARSELY CHOPPED
2 TABLESPOONS GRATED PARMESAN
CHEESE

1. In a large serving bowl, whisk together the basil, oil, lemon juice, mustard, lemon zest, salt, black pepper, and red pepper flakes. Set the dressing aside.

2. In a large pot of boiling water, cook the egg noodles with the whole garlic until the noodles are al dente according to package directions.

3. Meanwhile, place the peas and asparagus in a colander. When the noodles are done, drain them with the garlic in the colander (the hot water will thaw the vegetables). Rinse the noodles, garlic, and vegetables under cold running water and drain well. Cut the asparagus into ½-inch lengths.

4. Press the garlic cloves through a garlic press (or mash with a fork) and add them to the dressing. Whisk to blend well. Add the noodles, peas, asparagus, tomatoes, scallions, and Parmesan to the serving bowl, and toss well to coat with the dressing.

INDEX